Invited to dramatise several of Saʿdi's stories for radio, **Arthur Scholey** found himself wandering in delight in The Rose Garden, and The Orchard, among others of the poet and mystic's twenty-three books. Numerous tales and stories added to the fragrance of Saʿdi's flowers and fruit, and the re-told ones in The Discontented Dervishes (and its companion volume of Rumi stories, The Paragon Parrot) is the result – a taste, a scent, it is hoped, of the great works beyond.

This collection stems from Arthur Scholey's lifelong love of stories of all kinds – from folk tale, fable, sage, legend and parable, through to anecdote, joke and myths ancient and urban.

Collecting, creating and passing on stories, within today's fascinatingly burgeoning media, have led him to adapt others' and his own work in collections of his own and also for radio, tv, and stage performances. He also works with illustrators, and with composers on operas, dramatic cantatas and song collections.

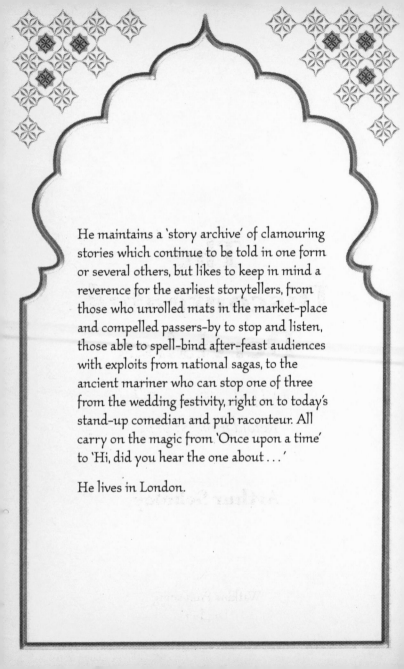

He maintains a 'story archive' of clamouring stories which continue to be told in one form or several others, but likes to keep in mind a reverence for the earliest storytellers, from those who unrolled mats in the market-place and compelled passers-by to stop and listen, those able to spell-bind after-feast audiences with exploits from national sagas, to the ancient mariner who can stop one of three from the wedding festivity, right on to today's stand-up comedian and pub raconteur. All carry on the magic from 'Once upon a time' to 'Hi, did you hear the one about . . .'

He lives in London.

The Discontented Dervishes

And Other Persian Tales
Retold from Sa'di by

Arthur Scholey

Watkins Publishing
London

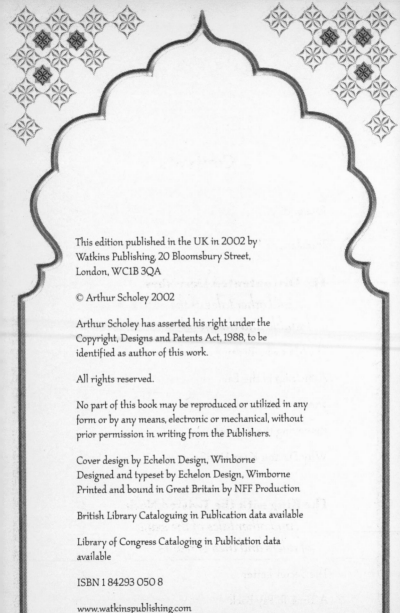

This edition published in the UK in 2002 by
Watkins Publishing, 20 Bloomsbury Street,
London, WC1B 3QA

© Arthur Scholey 2002

Cover design by Echelon Design, Wimborne
Designed and typeset by Echelon Design, Wimborne
Printed and bound in Great Britain by NFF Production

British Library Cataloguing in Publication data available

Library of Congress Cataloging in Publication data
available

ISBN 1 84293 050 8

www.watkinspublishing.com

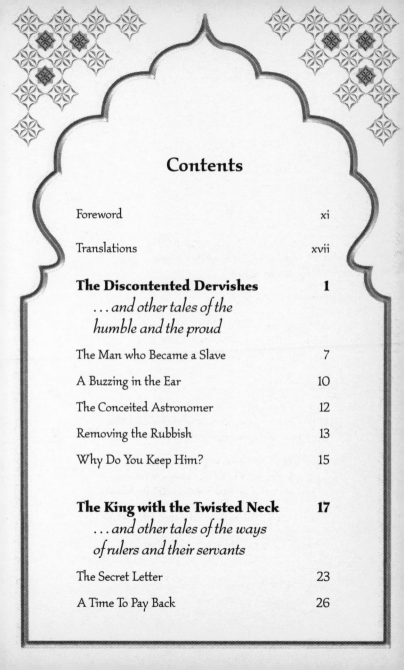

Contents

Contents

CONTENTS

Contents

CONTENTS

Contents

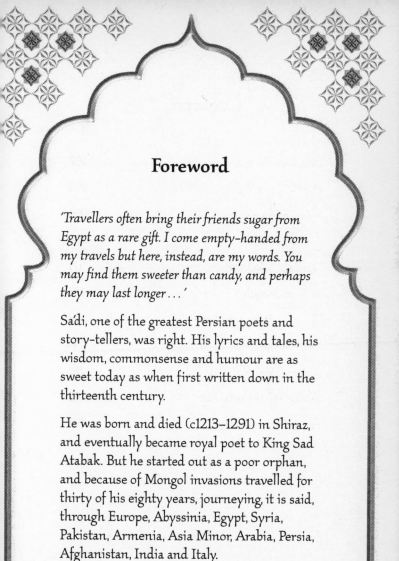

Foreword

'Travellers often bring their friends sugar from Egypt as a rare gift. I come empty-handed from my travels but here, instead, are my words. You may find them sweeter than candy, and perhaps they may last longer…'

Sa'di, one of the greatest Persian poets and story-tellers, was right. His lyrics and tales, his wisdom, commonsense and humour are as sweet today as when first written down in the thirteenth century.

He was born and died (c1213–1291) in Shiraz, and eventually became royal poet to King Sad Atabak. But he started out as a poor orphan, and because of Mongol invasions travelled for thirty of his eighty years, journeying, it is said, through Europe, Abyssinia, Egypt, Syria, Pakistan, Armenia, Asia Minor, Arabia, Persia, Afghanistan, India and Italy.

'Only once did I grumble at how Fortune had treated me. I was so poor that I could not even

afford shoes, and went into the mosque at Kiyah with a sore and complaining heart. There I saw a man with no feet . . .'

We do not have many details of his life. It is thought that his father died when Saʿdi was very young, particularly because he later wrote a moving poem about the love and care that should be shown to orphans. His desire to study drove him to the centre of learning at that time, Baghdad, but he was penniless and without influential friends. Then he managed to catch the ear of a wealthy resident, who generously provided funds for him to study at a private school where he stayed until he was twenty-one.

The next problem was how to enter the university. He wrote some verses and sent them off to the Professor of Literature at Nizamiah College, Baghdad. The verses pleased Shams-ud-din Abdul Farah (Saʿdi had considerately dedicated the verses to him) and he found himself helped financially again and admitted to the university. He worked hard and got a scholarship which enabled him to pursue his studies.

For the next forty-three years he stayed in Baghdad where he gained a reputation as a speaker and poet. He might have spent the rest of his life there, but the city was sacked. Sa'di fled for his life, and so began his travels, during which he even became a slave and was put to work in the trenches of Tripoli.

He was a Sufi, and it may be that throughout his journeys he wore the simple woollen robe of the followers of this way of life. The Arabic word 'suf' means 'wool' but also has a meaning connected with seeking the reality of things, the essence of life. The Sufis of Persia were of the faith of Islam, accepting the teachings of Mohammed, but essaying to go further in seeking the reality of God, trying to become one with him.

Sa'di married twice (the amusing story included here about his first wife should not perhaps be taken too literally!). He had a son who died when a child (see the final story in this collection), and a daughter who is said to have become the wife of another celebrated poet, Hafiz.

THE
DISCONTENTED DERVISHES

When he retired to his native Shiraz, he received royal patronage and wrote twenty-three books in all; the most famous of these are the Gulistan (The Rose Garden) and the Bustan (The Orchard). Into these he put the numerous stories he had both collected and made up, fragments from his own experiences, above all the wisdom of a lifetime, woven into the poetry.

While any poetry is difficult to translate (and, according to an Eastern saying, 'Each word of Sa'di has seventy-two meanings'!), the stories are part of the poetic structure of the books and I have concentrated on re-telling some of them. They range from healthy eating –

A king once asked a doctor how much he should eat daily.

'The weight of a hundred dirams,' the doctor said.

'Will this give me sufficient strength?' the king asked.

'It will carry you,' came the reply. 'If you eat more, you will have to carry it.'

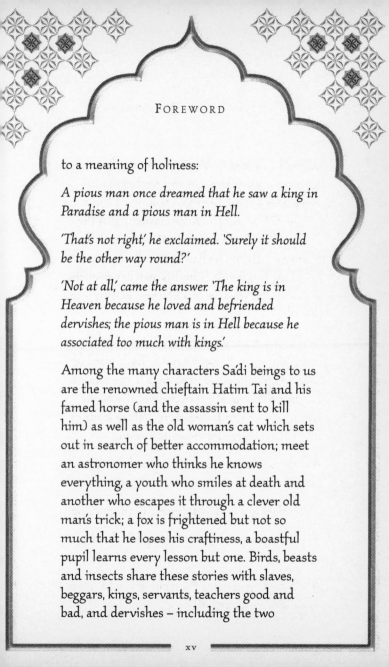

to a meaning of holiness:

A pious man once dreamed that he saw a king in Paradise and a pious man in Hell.

'That's not right,' he exclaimed. 'Surely it should be the other way round?'

'Not at all,' came the answer. 'The king is in Heaven because he loved and befriended dervishes; the pious man is in Hell because he associated too much with kings.'

Among the many characters Sa'di beings to us are the renowned chieftain Hatim Tai and his famed horse (and the assassin sent to kill him) as well as the old woman's cat which sets out in search of better accommodation; meet an astronomer who thinks he knows everything, a youth who smiles at death and another who escapes it through a clever old man's trick; a fox is frightened but not so much that he loses his craftiness, a boastful pupil learns every lesson but one. Birds, beasts and insects share these stories with slaves, beggars, kings, servants, teachers good and bad, and dervishes – including the two

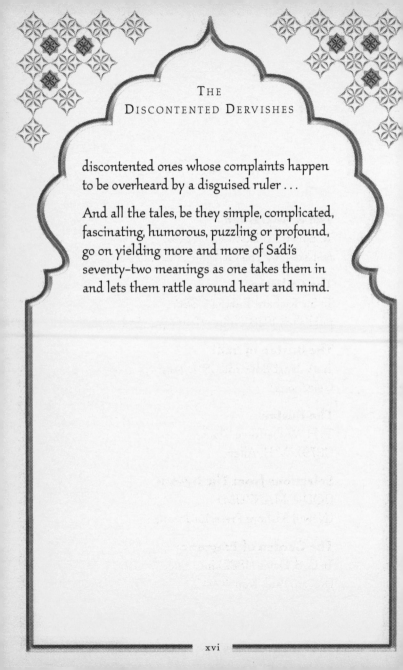

THE DISCONTENTED DERVISHES

discontented ones whose complaints happen to be overheard by a disguised ruler ...

And all the tales, be they simple, complicated, fascinating, humorous, puzzling or profound, go on yielding more and more of Saʿdī's seventy-two meanings as one takes them in and lets them rattle around heart and mind.

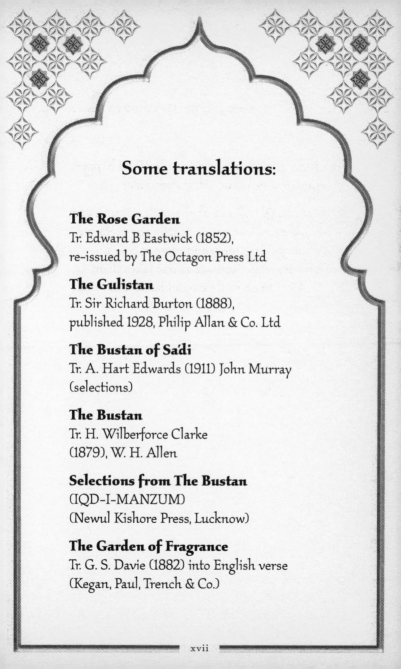

Some translations:

The Rose Garden
Tr. Edward B Eastwick (1852),
re-issued by The Octagon Press Ltd

The Gulistan
Tr. Sir Richard Burton (1888),
published 1928, Philip Allan & Co. Ltd

The Bustan of Sa'di
Tr. A. Hart Edwards (1911) John Murray
(selections)

The Bustan
Tr. H. Wilberforce Clarke
(1879), W. H. Allen

Selections from The Bustan
(IQD-I-MANZUM)
(Newul Kishore Press, Lucknow)

The Garden of Fragrance
Tr. G. S. Davie (1882) into English verse
(Kegan, Paul, Trench & Co.)

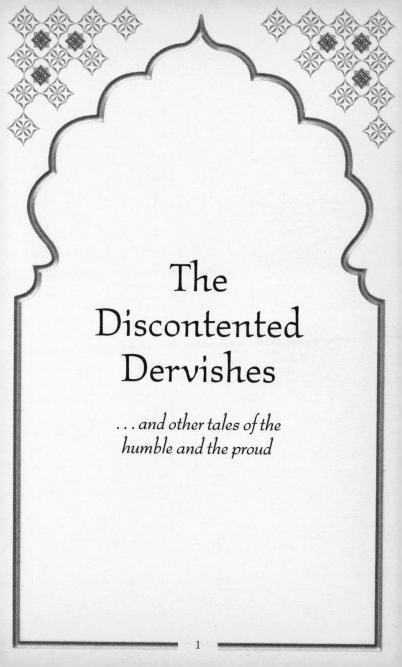

The Discontented Dervishes

... and other tales of the
humble and the proud

1

The Discontented Dervishes

K ING SALIH, one of the Kings of Syria, used to get up before dawn and walk about the streets and bazaars, heavily veiled like an Arab. He was renowned for his friendship with the poor and this was one of the ways he chose to find out about them and their problems.

Once, on one of these excursions, he stopped near a mosque. He had heard discontented voices coming from inside. He looked through the doorway without being noticed by the two dervishes sheltering there. They had no cloaks and had not been able to sleep all night because of the cold.

'There's no justice in this world,' said one. 'But we'll have satisfaction – on Judgment Day.'

'I hope so,' said the other, 'but I hope that those who have enjoyed this world get what they deserve as well. If I thought for one moment that kings, for example, who spend their lives

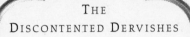

in sport, laughter and pleasure, got a place in Paradise – why, I believe I'd stop down here in my grave!'

'Don't worry,' said the first dervish, 'we'll get our reward – that's the point of our suffering now. As for rich and proud monarchs, well, they'll be the beggars in Paradise. And if we have no help from them in this life, I don't see why we should take the slightest pains to help them in the next when we shall be enjoying ourselves.'

'Neither do I,' replied the second dervish. 'Nevertheless, after a night such as we have just suffered, I can't help feeling angry. I do believe that if our King Salih were to walk through that door I should dash his brains out with my shoe!'

Understandably, King Salih decided that the moment had come to return to the palace. It was dawn by the time he arrived and immediately he sent a servant back to the mosque, with a message that the dervishes should come at once to the palace.

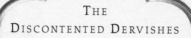

When the two dervishes arrived they found servants waiting. They were bathed and perfumed, given rich robes and ushered into the royal presence. The king, seated in magnificent splendour, smiled and indicated two places at table. The dervishes were astonished to find themselves among the highest nobility in the land.

So it was that the beggars, who had spent the night shivering in the cold and the rain, spent the day in warm luxury, dressed in robes of splendour and dining at the king's table.

When an opportunity occurred one of the dervishes approached the king.

'Great Monarch, whose commands are as a ring upon the ears of the world,' he began, 'we know, of course, that those approved of God naturally achieve greatness, but do tell us what it was in us poor slaves that particularly pleased you.'

The king's laughter made his face expand, like a rose, with pleasure.

'I hope you both see now,' he said, 'that I am not the sort of king who, in his grandeur, turns away his face from the helpless – that I am not, in fact, the monarch you abused in the mosque this morning. I beg you to change your ill-tempered view of me. I wouldn't like to think of any discord spoiling the Paradise to which you are going!

'Today, I opened to you the door of peace. I hope, when your time comes, you will not close it in my face?'

The Man Who Became a Slave

'*G*OT YOU!' cried the merchant, pouncing in triumph on a ragged unkempt man in the market place. 'I'll teach you to run away, slave! Put the chains on him, men. Now fellow, you'll pay for all the time and trouble I've had recapturing you.'

They dragged the unfortunate man off to Baghdad where the merchant was having himself a large house built. The slave was put to the hardest and dirtiest labour. He struggled to dig foundations in the clay. He dragged the stone, heaved the wood.

A year passed. Then, one morning, an abject starving wretch fell on his knees before the merchant.

'Forgive me, master,' he begged. 'I am your slave. I ran away a year ago.'

The merchant gasped in astonishment.

'But if you are my runaway slave,' he said,

'who is the man who has laboured in your place all these months?'

They rushed over to the building site, struck the chains off the man and brought him before the merchant.

'A terrible mistake has been made', cried the merchant. 'Please, tell me who you are.'

'My name', came the reply, 'is Lukman.'

'Lukman? Lukman! Oh, surely not Lukman, the renowned philosopher?'

'The same.'

The merchant fell on his knees. 'Mercy', he begged. 'Oh my dear sir, forgive me. Oh, how can I possibly recompense you? I beg you, have compassion!'

'Peace', said the philosopher, 'these apologies are of no use to me. For a year my heart has bled because of your severity – I can't forget that in an hour. But I do forgive you, so I beg you to get up.

'You see, we have both gained by this. Look,

you have your new house – and I have a
greater measure of God's Grace. I have a slave
of my own and I have often given him
difficult work to do. I'll never do it again. If I
ever even consider it, remembering this year
in your trenches will drive the thought from
my head!'

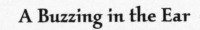

A Buzzing in the Ear

*H*AVE YOU HEARD that the famous Arabian chieftain, Hatim Tai, was deaf? Quite a few people believed that!

But, one morning, there was a fly buzzing as it struggled to escape from a spider's web. The spider had been so still and silent that the fly had perhaps thought it was a piece of sugar. Now it was about to learn otherwise.

Hatim Tai went over to the corner of the room where the buzzing was.

'You are caught by your own greediness,' he said to the fly. 'You won't find honey, sugar and candy in every nook and cranny. But that's where you will be certain to find traps and snares.' The buzzing stopped. The spider had its prey.

'But Hatim!' said a follower who had watched all this, 'how could you have possibly heard that fly? I could only just hear it myself. Yet everybody says you are deaf!'

'You're very clever,' said Hatim with a smile. 'Well, I see I must tell you about my deafness. It's like this: Much of my time, for reasons of state, I had to be among flatterers, the sort of people who hid my faults from me and filled my ears with praise. I couldn't help but take in some of their talk. I grew proud, and pride made me a wretched man.

'Then I gradually allowed them to think I was deaf. Naturally, there was much sad shaking of heads. But then came two great advantages.

'The first was that they stopped bothering to flatter me. They soon saw that it got them nowhere – all they had for their efforts was my blank face.

'The second was that I began to hear the truth about myself. When they thought I couldn't hear, they were quite frank about my good and my bad qualities. It was not always pleasant to hear my sins discussed publicly, but it quickly abolished my pride and helped me in avoiding further wickedness.'

The Conceited Astronomer

*O*NE WHO HAD A smattering of astronomy, yet believed that he knew it all, once travelled a great distance to see if he could possibly learn anything from the renowned philosopher, Abu-al-Hasan-Koshiyar.

With his heart full of desire and his head full of pride he came into the teacher's presence, sat and waited.

He waited a long time. Koshiyar did not acknowledge his presence; he closed his eyes and did not even raise his head.

At length, baffled and defeated, the man got up to go. At this, Koshiyar spoke.

'It is because you imagine yourself to be so full of knowledge that I can't teach you anything,' he said, 'for who can put more into a vessel that is already overflowing? You are full of yourself; that is why you must go empty of me.'

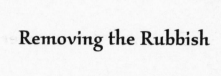

Removing the Rubbish

*W*HEN THE YOUNG TRAVELLER got off the boat, they saw that he looked so wise, devout and humble that there was only one place at which he could possibly stay.

They deposited his luggage at the monastery. There the youth was made welcome by the pious community.

One day the head of the community said to the youth:

'Would you please sweep the rubbish away from the mosque?'

That was the last they saw of him. All were puzzled, but decided that he had no aptitude for work.

But next day, one of the servants of the community happened to catch sight of the youth, and stopped him.

'It was foolish of you to go off like that,' he

remarked. 'Don't you know that it is only by service that you climb the ladder?'

At this the youth wept.

'Oh my friend,' he cried, 'what could I do? I looked around and the place was spotless. I therefore concluded that the head of the community was referring to me! I removed myself so that the place should remain pure and spotless.'

Why Do You Keep Him?

'THAT SLAVE OF YOURS!' complained a friend to a wise man, 'why do you put up with him? What a sight he is. He's dirty, his hair is dishevelled, and have you ever seen such a sour face? He's got teeth like a serpent's and they look just as poisonous. If there was a prize for ugliness, he would walk off with it!'

All this was true, yet only part of it. The slave had some disease of the eyes which caused them to run continually. And, because he never washed, he didn't smell too wholesome, either.

When it was time to do the cooking, the slave just sat there with a frown. When the meal was brought in he took a place next to his master but it never entered his head that it might be his job to serve him. His master could have died before the slave offered him even a glass of water.

They had tried talking to him. It had no effect. They had beaten him, with the same result.

Night and day there always seemed to be
trouble over him. He threw thorns and
rubbish in the road. He flung hens down the
well. Everyone was frightened of him; he
looked so wild. When he was sent out on
errands, it took him ages to get back.

'Now, tell me,' continued the wise man's friend,
'what do you expect to get from him? Is it
manners? Some skill or other? It can't be
beauty. Is he worth anything to you when you
have to endure his violent behaviour? It's a
continual torment. Now, let me get you a
decent slave, and take this creature back to the
dealer. If anything is offered for him, take it,
however small. It will be well worth it to be rid
of him. Now what do you say?'

The wise man smiled. 'I am grateful to you,
my friend,' he replied. 'The slave does have a
bad nature – but the fact is that he is helping
to make mine good. If I can learn to put up
with him, then I can put up with anyone!'

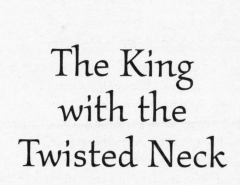

The King
with the
Twisted Neck

*. . . and other tales of the ways of
rulers and their servants*

The King with the Twisted Neck

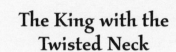

THE GREAT WARRIOR KING was heading a magnificent procession through the crowded city when, suddenly, the jubilant cheers changed to cries of horror. The royal black horse reared up, startled, and the king fell, hitting his head on a stone jar.

Fearfully the servants approached his still body. What relief! He was alive. They carried him back to the palace.

But in the following days, there was increasing cause for concern. In falling, the king had twisted a bone in his neck. Try as he might he could not now move his head. It sat on his neck as still as an elephant's. If he wanted to turn he had to move his whole body.

'Where are my doctors?' he whined. 'Where are the famed physicians of my land? Send out for the surgeons.'

They came from near and far. But all their remedies, all their suggestions were useless. The king was in great agony if anyone so much as touched his neck.

The search for a doctor went on; for all knew that the king would soon be paralysed as the twisted bone was pressing on a vein in his neck.

One day an insignificant-looking Greek doctor arrived at the palace and asked to be admitted to the king. He was allowed to examine the royal neck. Then he announced that he could cure the king. He was naturally given permission to proceed at once.

The Greek doctor jumped on the king, caught his head in a firm grip and pressed at the same time with his feet on the king's shoulders. The royal agony was heard all over the palace. Servants rushed in. Guards appeared with drawn swords.

They were just about to kill the poor doctor when the king cried: 'Stop!'

He rose up with an ecstatic smile. To everyone's astonishment, he moved his head easily from side to side. Cheers broke out. The king was restored.

In all the excitement, no one remembered the Greek doctor. He hung about at the edge of the joyful crowd hoping, at least, for a good word. In the end, he slunk unhappily away.

Next day, there was another glorious procession. Rapturous cheers greeted the king as he rode through the city, turning his head easily to left and right to acknowledge the applause of his subjects.

The Greek doctor had found himself a spot where he knew that the king must notice him. He waited, sure that the king would recognise and reward him.

When the time came, the king saw the doctor, but turned his head away.

'Had I not cured him yesterday, he would not have been able to do that to me today,' said the

doctor sadly as he went home. He took out a box of special seeds and called his slave.

'Take these to the palace', he ordered, 'and with them these written instructions'.

The slave did as he had been ordered. The king received the seeds and read the instructions which said:

'To get the full benefit, burn these seeds on the perfume censer'.

The instructions were carried out. The king leaned forward to sniff the scent that arose, sneezed – and dislocated his neck. He howled in agony and dismay. He was just as he was before the Greek doctor had attended him.

'Find him!' he groaned. 'That Greek doctor. I know he's still in the city. Get him here. Offer him what he asks. Offer him more than he asks. But get him here now!'

They searched the city. They searched the whole country, and beyond.

The Greek doctor was never found.

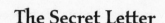

The Secret Letter

E VERYONE LIKED THE chief minister
at the court of the King of Zuzan. He was
courteous and gracious to everyone he met;
and he never said one thing to a man's face
and another behind his back.

However, it once happened that the king
became displeased with him for something he
was supposed to have done. He was accused,
convicted, fined and put into prison.

He was well treated while he was there. The
prison officials remembered how kind he had
been in the past. They were courteous and
gracious in return. No harsh treatment was
allowed, and no insults came his way.

In time he was acquitted of some of the
accusations against him, but not all of them,
and he still languished in prison.

One day, a secret letter was smuggled in to
him. It came from the king of a neighbouring
country, and said:

Far from appreciating your many excellent qualities, the King of Zuzan rewards you with disgrace. If, at any time, you were to think of coming here, we can assure you of very different treatment. We, and all our nobles, would be delighted to welcome you. We await your answer.

The imprisoned minister was alarmed by this letter. Suppose it was discovered that he had received a secret message from a neighbouring king? Suppose it was a plot? He felt himself to be in very great danger. He thought for some time, then wrote a brief message on the back of the letter and pushed it back to the guard who had smuggled it in. From the small window of his cell he saw a courier leave.

All this had been carefully watched by one of the king's courtiers, and when it was reported to the king, he was very angry. He sent swift messengers who caught up with the courier, and brought him back. The king was handed the secret letter. He read the message from the neighbouring king, and on the back of it he read his minister's reply:

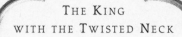

I don't deserve your Highness' high opinion of me and I cannot accept your invitation. All my life my Royal Master has been kind and generous and though it is true that, at the moment, he does not seem too pleased with me, yet I cannot be ungrateful. It is written: When someone has given you favour upon favour, you can surely overlook a single injury.

The king was moved by what he read. He sent for his minister, dressed him in a robe of honour, gave him presents and gold, and then said publicly:

'I believe now that you are innocent, and that I have caused you much suffering. I ask you to pardon me.'

'There is nothing to pardon, my lord,' said the minister, gracious and courteous as ever. 'It is obviously the will of God on High that I should suffer some misfortune. That being so, I would rather have had it from your generous hand than anyone else's.'

A Time To Pay Back

A HIGH-RANKING and proud official of the king once threw a stone and hit the head of a poor dervish. The official laughed and rode on. Overawed, the dervish had no power to retaliate.

But a time came when the king was angry with the official. He took away his position and his riches, had him bound and thrown into a muddy pit where all could see his disgrace.

The poor dervish called down to him: 'Do you recall a day when you threw a stone at me?'

'I do not,' said the prisoner. 'It must have been a long time ago. And why do you bother me with such matters now?'

'At that time,' said the dervish, 'I was overawed by your splendour. But now that I see you in this condition, I am able to take advantage of it.' He delved into his rags and produced a stone.

'This is the same stone that I have saved all this while,' he said, and he threw it at the head of the once-proud man.

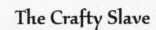

The Crafty Slave

A SLAVE, BELONGING TO the Sultan Umrulais, escaped and ran away. Servants were quickly sent in pursuit. He didn't get far. They caught him, brought him back, and threw him in chains at the feet of the sultan.

'Make an example of him', said the vizier, who had a grudge against the slave. 'Have him executed, my lord, or you'll have all the slaves trying to escape.'

The slave fell to the ground before Umrulais. 'O Sultan', he said, 'if you want my head off there's nothing I can do about it. However, you haven't been a bad master. You've fed me well and on the whole I've been happy. So I should be sorry if, on the Day of Resurrection, you were punished for illegally shedding my blood. If you must kill me, do it according to the law.'

'Indeed?' said the Sultan. 'Suppose you tell me how I could do that?'

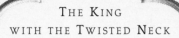

'Well,' said the slave, 'here's one way, for example: the law says it is perfectly all right to kill in retaliation for another death. Now if you were to give me permission to kill your vizier here, you could then execute me legally without any fear.'

The sultan laughed and turned to the vizier. 'What do you say to that?' he asked.

The vizier groaned and raised his eyes to heaven. 'It's my fault,' he sighed. 'I should have remembered the saying: If you shoot an arrow at your foe, don't forget you are also a sitting target for him. My lord, rather than get myself into any further danger, I beg you to let the rascal go!'

The Boy Who Smiled at Death

*T*HERE WAS ONCE A KING who fell ill of a nasty disease. I won't give you the details, except to say that they were horrible and he was in great pain. All sorts of remedies were tried, without success. In the end, when the king was near to death, the doctors finally agreed that there was only one remedy. But this involved obtaining the liver and gall of a person with special qualities.

They produced the list of qualities and began to read them out. Halfway through the reading, the King stopped them.

'There is so little time', he gasped. 'If there is such a person, with all these qualities, he must be got here as soon as possible. The quicker you set about it the better.'

Messengers sped through the kingdom. Days passed, but no one could be found who had all the qualities on the doctors' list.

Then, at last, in a remote part, a messenger

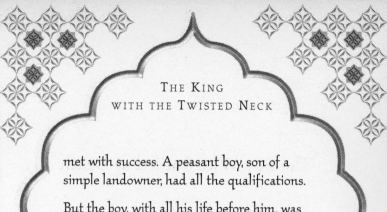

met with success. A peasant boy, son of a simple landowner, had all the qualifications.

But the boy, with all his life before him, was horrified at the thought of death, even though this would benefit his king. His parents were also horrified, at first. But their eyes widened, as, one by one, bags of gold were piled up before them. At last they stopped shaking their heads, and nodded.

At this the boy cried out to them in despair. They turned sadly away.

As he was being taken to the palace, the boy suddenly thought: 'There is surely a law against the spilling of innocent blood? I will appeal to the qazi.'

The qazi said: 'True, there is such a law – but it is set aside in circumstances such as these. It is permissible to spill blood if, by so doing, the king's life can be saved.' He signed the deed of execution.

The boy was brought before the king. Standing by the throne were the doctors and the

executioner with his knife. The boy thought: 'Any subject is supposed to be able to appeal to the king for justice,' but when he saw the pain-racked king he knew there was no hope for him there.

Then the boy looked up to heaven and smiled. The king was amazed. 'How can you smile when you are about to die?' he asked.

'What else can I do?' said the youth. 'I appealed to my mother and father, but they did not help me; their love has been overcome by gold. And the qazi, to whom your subjects are supposed to bring complaints, has instead issued the decree for my execution. As a final resort, subjects can approach the king, but I see that it is useless to appeal to you for justice, since it is through my death that you seek to save your life. There is no other help for me, then, but in God most high. And that is why I smile, for I know that He, surely, remains true when all others fail, and He will therefore protect me.'

The king wept with shame and said: 'It is better for me to die than shed innocent blood.'

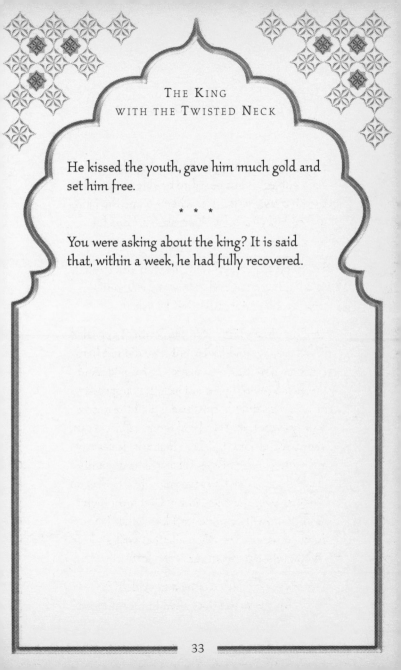

THE KING
WITH THE TWISTED NECK

He kissed the youth, gave him much gold and
set him free.

* * *

You were asking about the king? It is said
that, within a week, he had fully recovered.

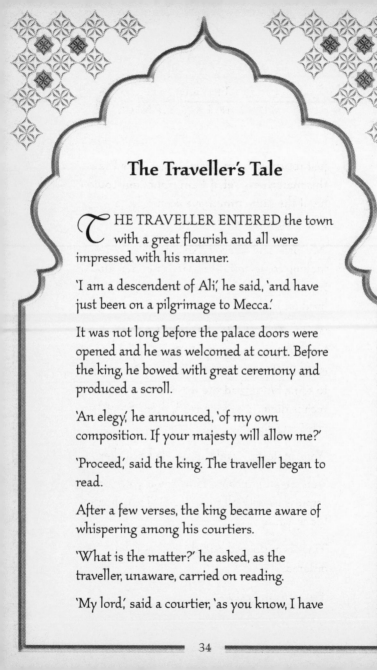

The Traveller's Tale

*T*HE TRAVELLER ENTERED the town
with a great flourish and all were
impressed with his manner.

'I am a descendent of Ali,' he said, 'and have
just been on a pilgrimage to Mecca.'

It was not long before the palace doors were
opened and he was welcomed at court. Before
the king, he bowed with great ceremony and
produced a scroll.

'An elegy,' he announced, 'of my own
composition. If your majesty will allow me?'

'Proceed,' said the king. The traveller began to
read.

After a few verses, the king became aware of
whispering among his courtiers.

'What is the matter?' he asked, as the
traveller, unaware, carried on reading.

'My lord,' said a courtier, 'as you know, I have

just returned from Bosrah. I am sure I saw this man there. Yet, if I am right, how could he, at the same time, have been on a pilgrimage to Mecca?'

'My lord', said a second courtier, 'I have been making some enquiries. He is not descended from Ali at all. His father was a Christian and lived on Malta.'

'And look, my lord', said a third, holding out a book, 'this is a copy of the Diwan by the justly celebrated poet Anvari. See, here!' He pointed to some lines, 'read the words as this man recites them.' The king read, then, 'Stop!' he cried angrily.

'Your majesty?' said the startled traveller.

'You are an imposter! How could you hope to impress us with all these lies?' He turned to his servants.

'Have him flogged and thrown out', he ordered.

'But your majesty – '

35

'I'll hear no more.'

'One word, I beg, if you will allow me. If that word is not the truth then I deserve all the punishment you can give me.'

'Well? Go on.'

The traveller recited:

> 'Cream, from a poor man, is a mere
> Cup of milk in a water-filled pail.
> Take no offence, then, for you'll hear
> As little truth in a traveller's tale.'

The king laughed. 'The truest words you have spoken,' he said. 'All right, release him. And prepare a gift for him.'

O King, Live For Ever!

*L*ET ME TELL YOU about the excellent vizier that King Faridun had. He served God first, and then the king, faithfully and efficiently carrying out every command to perfection.

He was also wise, far-seeing and clever – all qualities which stood him in good stead when one day someone spoke privately to the king:

'Your majesty, may all your days be easy and all your wishes granted; it goes without saying that I speak only because I feel it is my duty to do so, and from no other motive than a desire for your continued well-being.'

'Go on.'

'It is ... er ... delicate, to say the least, but ... your vizier, excellent though he may be – and few would dispute it – yet I very much regret to say that he is, in secret, your enemy.'

'I find that difficult to believe,' said the king.

'What evidence do you have?'

'You know, of course, that he lends his wealth to any who ask for it?'

'I do, and there is nothing wrong with that.'

'Are you aware that nearly everyone in the army is indebted to him, that there are few – from the highest officers to the lowest ranks – who do not owe him money? And with this clause in the agreements – that all money owed should be returned to the vizier on the instant that your majesty dies.'

'A strange clause,' said the king, growing pale.

'What else can that mean but that your vizier thinks constantly of your death, since it is only when that happens that he can get his money back?'

The king brooded on this for a long time. He was loathe to believe that his vizier was secretly anticipating his death while publicly, and often, desiring that he should live for ever. At last, and in court, the king could not restrain himself any longer.

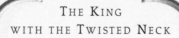

'Vizier!' he called, 'Among all my friends gathered here, why is it that you, in your heart, are my secret enemy?'

The vizier was astonished. The king immediately poured out all he knew of the vizier's activities and the conclusion to be drawn from them.

At this the vizier knelt and kissed the ground before the throne.

'O renowned and royal master,' he said, 'since you have discovered this secret, let me also reveal to you the reason for it.'

'Well, proceed.'

'It is simply that when I wish you long life, I like to think that everyone else is as sincere as I am! Now that the world knows that I shall demand the return of my silver at your death, they will, like me, honestly wish you to live for ever!'

The king laughed, delighted with the answer. He rewarded the vizier with an even higher office, and greater dignity at court.

The Good Lie

T HE KING WAS ANGRY with the foreign captive who had been thrown down before him.

'Put him to death!' he ordered.

The captive had been expecting it. He had up to now been silent but, now that death was certain, he gave up all hope and cursed the king, using the foulest words in his native tongue. He was like a cat, spitting and screeching at dogs who are at its throat.

The king, not knowing the language, did not understand what the captive was screaming, but he knew that one or two of his viziers were familiar with the tongue.

'What is he saying?' he asked them.

The viziers looked at each other. Then, one, who was good-natured, replied: 'My lord, he is quoting from the sacred Koran.'

'Indeed?' said the king. 'From which verse?'

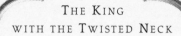

The vizier went on: 'From the verse which speaks of the Paradise which awaits those who control their anger and forgive, for God loves men of goodwill.'

'I see,' said the king, thoughtfully. He turned to the now silent captive. 'You have done well to remind me of that,' he said. 'I will control my anger. And I will forgive you. You can go free.'

'That was disgraceful!' muttered another vizier, an enemy and rival of the one who had replied to the king's question. 'People of our rank should speak nothing but the truth, particularly before the king.'

The king overheard. 'What was that?' he asked.

'My lord!' protested the second vizier, 'I am sorry, but you were told a lie by that vizier! The captive was certainly not quoting from the Koran. The truth is that he was pouring foul abuse and the filthiest of insults upon you!'

The king frowned at this. 'Then I prefer his lie

41

to your truth!' he said. 'I think that your truth
came from a heart bent upon mischief. His lie
came from a good heart, and good has come of
it, as you have seen.'

A Picture of an Enemy

SCARCELY ABLE TO CRAWL, the old traveller inched his way painfully along the river bank and collapsed at the gate of the city. He was dirty, in rags, and feverish.

Fortunately for him the king in that part was a kind man, with a reputation for befriending strangers and the poor. His servants, always on the lookout for ways of carrying out his wishes, caught sight of the exhausted traveller. They took him in, washed him and tended to his needs. He was given clean clothes and food.

As he recovered, he told the servants of his travels. He had journeyed throughout Turkey, Arabia, Greece and Persia. He had talked with learned men, gathered knowledge of many branches of science, observed different societies and classes. The servants were pleased when a man of his experience spoke well of their own country. It was not long before the king himself asked to see him.

THE
DISCONTENTED DERVISHES

'I should like to hear about where you are from and of your travels,' said the king, when greetings had been exchanged, 'but, first of all, I am most eager to hear what is your opinion of this country.'

'I have nothing but praise for both it and for you, great king,' the traveller replied. 'The people are contented and I have seen no one afflicted in any way. A sign of a good country is that people have no need to get drunk. Here, your taverns seem to be almost out of business!'

Naturally, the king was pleased. He thanked the traveller, and presented him with gifts. If he suspected flattery, his suspicions were dispelled, during the many pleasurable conversations that followed, when he heard something of the man's vast experience of the world's kingdoms. The traveller told him where he was born, of his education, and of how, during his journeyings, he acquired his knowledge, science and politics. The king soon began to think that the man would make a better vizier than the one he had. He was

tempted to make an immediate appointment,
but he decided it would be much better to
elevate the man gradually; then more of his
court would come to know him, and no one
would be offended.

As time passed, the king became absolutely
convinced of his assessment of the man. He
was wise, considerate, thoughtful, tactful and a
good judge of men.

The king felt he need be cautious no longer,
and the appointment was announced. He
made the man chief vizier, over the one who
up to now had held the office.

It proved to be a good appointment. The man
knew how to do his job with real skill. He was
knowledgeable, efficient and he organised
matters so well that most people were glad to
have him in charge.

There were, of course, a few unhappy people.
These were the envious, and they were
miserable because they could find nothing
deceitful in the new vizier, and consequently
no way in which they could slander him.

But the former vizier never gave up. He was always spying on the man, desperate to find some way of injuring him. In the end, he succeeded.

The King had two handsome young slaves, so alike that one was a reflection of the other. These, as did everyone else at the court, liked to listen whenever the vizier spoke. When they saw that he seemed particularly friendly towards them, they, in turn, became his allies and well-wishers. And the vizier looked at their faces often, in quiet delight.

This relationship was just what the former vizier wanted. Eventually he appeared before the king.

'I hesitate to bother you, my lord,' he said. 'I don't really know this new vizier, or even where he is from. However, it is well-known that those who journey from country to country have no respect or fear for any single one of them. In this case, it is time that you were informed of some suspicions about him. He has an unnatural, and possibly treacherous, affection

for two of your slaves. It has been known for some time, but I did not feel able to come to you until I was sure. But now I have the evidence of one of my attendants who actually caught the vizier embracing one of the boys. Well, my lord, after all my years in your service, I couldn't remain silent for ever. Now that I have told you I can leave it safely in your hands.'

It only takes a few twigs to start a fire, but once it is going, the whole tree can be burnt. The king blazed with anger at this revelation, though outwardly he appeared calm. He told himself that his new vizier had risen by his own royal favour and that it would be utterly wrong to cause his downfall merely on the evidence of another's suspicion.

Nevertheless, he began to watch the vizier more closely. And it was not long before he saw him glance at one of the slaves, and the slave furtively grinned back. It was an exchange that needed no words, and one that instantly confirmed the king's suspicions. His anger burned again but still he kept outwardly calm as he called the vizier over.

'O, one of good name', he said, 'I thought you
were wise and intelligent and that any state
secrets would be safe in your hands. But now I
hear that which makes me find you shameless
and unworthy, and certainly unfit to be in the
highest office in the land. You are not entirely
to blame. It is my responsibility, my sin, if I
foster treachery in my own house.'

The vizier raised his head. 'O King', he said, 'I
know myself to be without guilt of any kind,
and have nothing of any baseness in my heart.
What have you heard?'

'It was my former vizier who opened my eyes',
said the king. At this the vizier could hardly
conceal a smile.

'It does not surprise me', he said, 'You, O King,
placed me above him, so from that hour he
became my enemy. He will be my enemy until
doomsday, for when I am honoured so he
must be disgraced. Permit me, Lord, to tell you
a story:

'I read in a book somewhere about a man
who dreamed he saw Satan – and he was

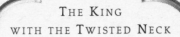

magnificent! He was tall and proud as a forest pine, glowing with light as if he were the sun itself.

"O wonderful being," cried the dreamer, "can you really be Satan? Surely, even the angels are not as beautiful as this? How can we ever have imagined you to be ugly? You should see the caricatures of you on the toilet walls! And even in the king's palace you are depicted as dejected and ugly as Sa – well, ugly anyway!"

"Well," said Satan, "you are fortunate in being granted a vision of me as I really am, and you can see that I am not as ugly as – as I am painted. The fact is that you must now agree that those who drew me, on toilet or palace walls, must have been my enemies! Ever since I threw Adam out of Paradise, his sons have drawn me ugly. It is sheer malice!"

'And so you see, my lord, why this man, your former vizier, will never draw a good picture of me. If I am bold in speech, forgive me. It is because I know I am free from baseness'.

The king was momentarily puzzled. Boldness

THE
DISCONTENTED DERVISHES

of speech, he knew, could equally be the mark
of a guilty man. He spoke again.

'My charge against you does not come solely
from him,' he said. 'I have the evidence of my
own eyes! Of all the people in my court – and
look at them – why have you eyes only for
these two slaves?'

Once again the vizier smiled.

'That is true,' he said, 'and I have no real wish
to hide it. My lord, it is a subtle point but if
you will permit me to attempt to explain? It's
like this. You can't have failed to notice how a
beggar looks at those who are rich. Well, I am
that beggar in relation to these boys, for see
how rich they are in the currency of youth!
Then see how all my riches are gone, spent in
play and pastime. Sometimes I can hardly
bear to look at them – they have so much
capital in grace and beauty. Would you believe
it, my lord, that I once had a rose-coloured
face like theirs? That my limbs too shone like
crystal? I look at their black curls and feel it is
time to spin my shroud when I contemplate

50

my own ragged strands. Yes, I was well-proportioned like them, but now look at my spindle of a body! See, they smile with teeth like silver pearls. As I speak, have pity on me – see my teeth, fallen in like old city walls.

'Is it not permissible then, to steal an occasional glance at these two, to recall my mis-spent youth, to remember in my old age, those precious, precious days?'

The king smiled. 'You could not have made a better answer,' he said. He turned to this court. 'You will never hear anything more beautiful and true than this. There can be nothing reprehensible in a man who can offer so good an explanation of his behaviour. To think that, had I not been cautious, I might have injured him through the word of his enemy.'

He rewarded him with further gifts, and publicly rebuked the former vizier.

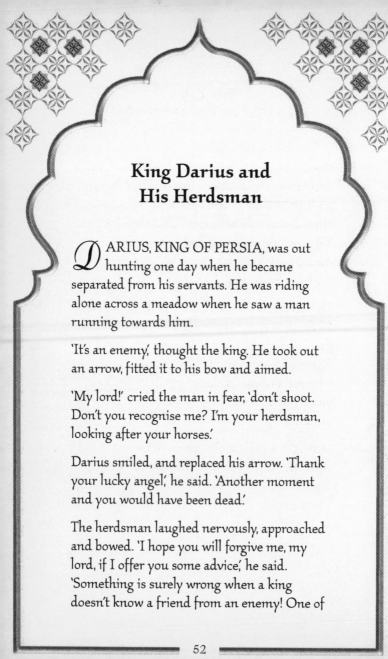

King Darius and His Herdsman

DARIUS, KING OF PERSIA, was out
hunting one day when he became
separated from his servants. He was riding
alone across a meadow when he saw a man
running towards him.

'It's an enemy', thought the king. He took out
an arrow, fitted it to his bow and aimed.

'My lord!' cried the man in fear, 'don't shoot.
Don't you recognise me? I'm your herdsman,
looking after your horses.'

Darius smiled, and replaced his arrow. 'Thank
your lucky angel', he said. 'Another moment
and you would have been dead.'

The herdsman laughed nervously, approached
and bowed. 'I hope you will forgive me, my
lord, if I offer you some advice', he said.
'Something is surely wrong when a king
doesn't know a friend from an enemy! One of

the conditions of your high place is that you
should know every one of your dependants. I
have often been in your presence. We have
often discussed the horses that I tend for you.
Yet now, when I ran joyfully across the
meadow to greet you, you couldn't recognise
me from an enemy.'

The herdsman spread his arms wide. 'You see
all these horses? There are a hundred
thousand of them! Yet I know every one.
Name one, and I will bring it to you. That's
why you put me in charge of them. O King,
you should tend your own flock with the
same care.'

Darius, it is said, spoke kindly to the man, and
wrote the advice in his heart.

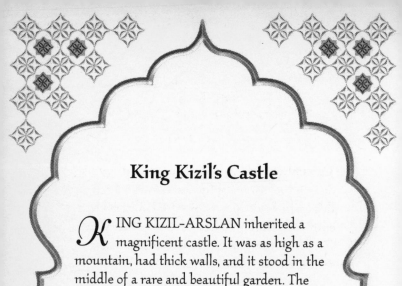

King Kizil's Castle

*K*ING KIZIL-ARSLAN inherited a magnificent castle. It was as high as a mountain, had thick walls, and it stood in the middle of a rare and beautiful garden. The ways to the castle were narrow and twisting and so it was easily defended. The king rested, secure, with no cares.

One day, a wise man journeyed the long and tedious path to visit the king. He had travelled the world and seen its marvels. The king made him welcome and feasted him.

'In all your travels', said the king, 'tell me, have you seen a castle such as this, a fortress so protected so strong?'

The wise man smiled, 'Your castle is beautiful', he replied, 'but not strong enough.'

'How so?' the king asked.

'Have not others held the castle before you?' asked the wise man.

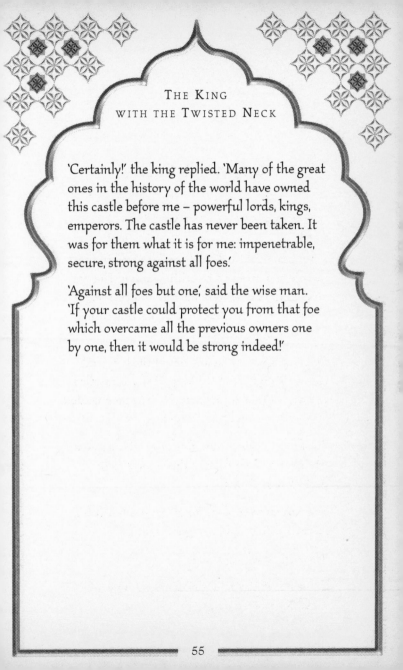

The King
with the Twisted Neck

'Certainly!' the king replied. 'Many of the great ones in the history of the world have owned this castle before me – powerful lords, kings, emperors. The castle has never been taken. It was for them what it is for me: impenetrable, secure, strong against all foes.'

'Against all foes but one,' said the wise man. 'If your castle could protect you from that foe which overcame all the previous owners one by one, then it would be strong indeed!'

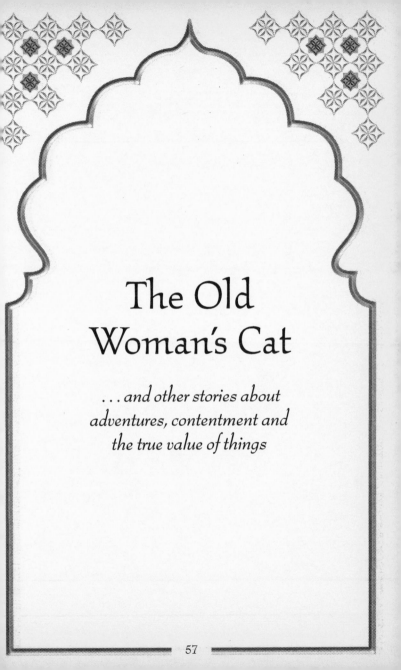

The Old Woman's Cat

*. . . and other stories about
adventures, contentment and
the true value of things*

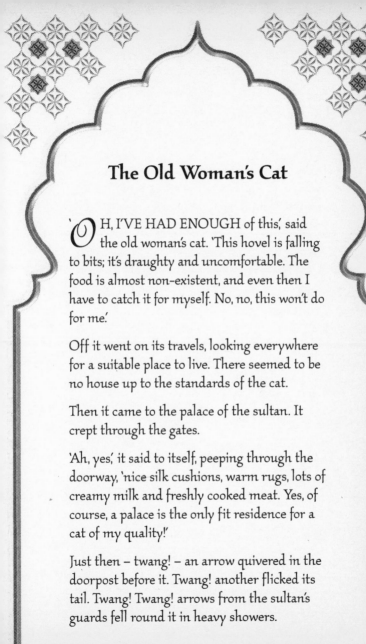

The Old Woman's Cat

'*O*H, I'VE HAD ENOUGH of this,' said the old woman's cat. 'This hovel is falling to bits; it's draughty and uncomfortable. The food is almost non-existent, and even then I have to catch it for myself. No, no, this won't do for me.'

Off it went on its travels, looking everywhere for a suitable place to live. There seemed to be no house up to the standards of the cat.

Then it came to the palace of the sultan. It crept through the gates.

'Ah, yes,' it said to itself, peeping through the doorway, 'nice silk cushions, warm rugs, lots of creamy milk and freshly cooked meat. Yes, of course, a palace is the only fit residence for a cat of my quality!'

Just then – twang! – an arrow quivered in the doorpost before it. Twang! another flicked its tail. Twang! Twang! arrows from the sultan's guards fell round it in heavy showers.

'Yeowww!' screamed the cat. Howling and bleeding, it fled across the palace yard. But the arrows followed. Soon the cat was in a sorry state.

'Mercy!' it sobbed, dodging through the gates. 'If only I get out of this alive, that old woman's shack – and just an occasional small mouse – are all I shall ever desire!'

Food Fit for a King

A KING ONCE ASKED an Arabian doctor how much he should eat daily.

'The weight of a hundred dirams,' the doctor said.

'Will this give me sufficient strength?' the king asked.

'It will carry you,' came the reply. 'If you eat more, you will have to carry *it*.'

Market Value

I SAW AN ARAB MERCHANT sitting among some jewellers at Basrah. He told them this story: 'I once lost my way in the desert. Soon I had eaten every scrap of food and I knew that I was not far from death. In despair, I searched again through my luggage and found a bag which felt to me as if it were full of grain. You can imagine my joy, my absolute ecstasy!

'Imagine my despair and bitterness, then, when I got the bag open. It was full of pearls.'

I Once Complained

*O*NLY ONCE DID I EVER grumble at how Fortune treated me. I was so poor that I could not even afford shoes, and went into the mosque at Kufah with a sore and complaining heart. There I saw a man with no feet.

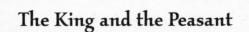

The King and the Peasant

A KING AND HIS COURTIERS were enjoying a winter hunt but, as dusk fell, they realised they were far from any suitable place to spend the night. As it grew darker, all they could find was a peasant's cottage.

'Let us see if we can stay there', suggested the king, 'for it is certainly very cold.'

His vizier protested: 'You can't spend the night in the hut of a miserable peasant, my lord! It would lower your royal dignity. Let us pitch our tents, light many fires, and make the best of it.'

Inside his cottage, the peasant had heard all this. He quickly came out and kissed the ground before the king.

'I am sure that your royal dignity would not be lowered if you stayed in my hut', he said, 'I suspect that your vizier is more worried that my peasant dignity might be raised a little.'

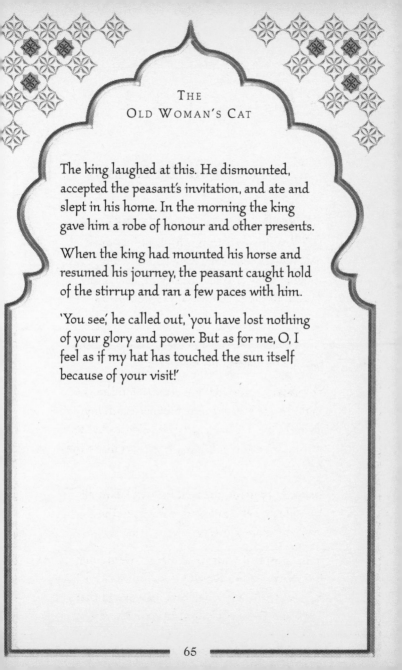

THE
OLD WOMAN'S CAT

The king laughed at this. He dismounted, accepted the peasant's invitation, and ate and slept in his home. In the morning the king gave him a robe of honour and other presents.

When the king had mounted his horse and resumed his journey, the peasant caught hold of the stirrup and ran a few paces with him.

'You see,' he called out, 'you have lost nothing of your glory and power. But as for me, O, I feel as if my hat has touched the sun itself because of your visit!'

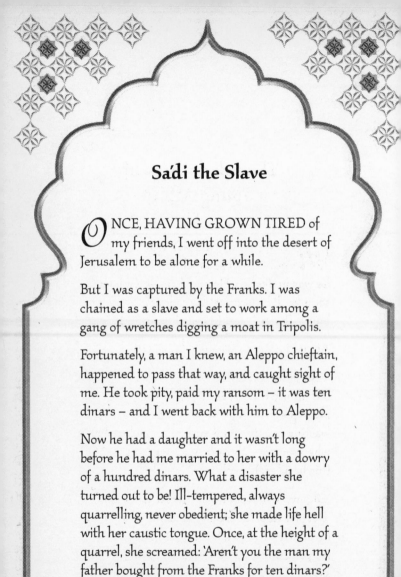

Sa'di the Slave

ONCE, HAVING GROWN TIRED of my friends, I went off into the desert of Jerusalem to be alone for a while.

But I was captured by the Franks. I was chained as a slave and set to work among a gang of wretches digging a moat in Tripolis.

Fortunately, a man I knew, an Aleppo chieftain, happened to pass that way, and caught sight of me. He took pity, paid my ransom – it was ten dinars – and I went back with him to Aleppo.

Now he had a daughter and it wasn't long before he had me married to her with a dowry of a hundred dinars. What a disaster she turned out to be! Ill-tempered, always quarrelling, never obedient; she made life hell with her caustic tongue. Once, at the height of a quarrel, she screamed: 'Aren't you the man my father bought from the Franks for ten dinars?'

'Yes,' I replied. 'He bought me for ten dinars and sold me to you for a hundred!'

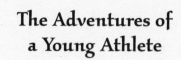

The Adventures of
a Young Athlete

*H*E WAS A STRONG YOUNG athlete but he had such a lot of bad luck that he was in despair. He couldn't get a job and soon he did not have even enough money to buy sufficient food to keep his strength up.

At last he went miserably to his father.

'I think the best thing for me', he said, 'is to set out on my travels, don't you? Surely with my physique I could get a job somewhere. I'm wasting my time and energy cooped up here where no one can see my good qualities. Will this be all right with you?'

'Oh, my son, no it won't', his father replied. 'Do, please, put this silly idea out of your head. My dear boy, try and be content. I won't let you starve, you know that. Remember the saying: Exertion will bring neither riches nor wealth; in times of want, moderate your desires.'

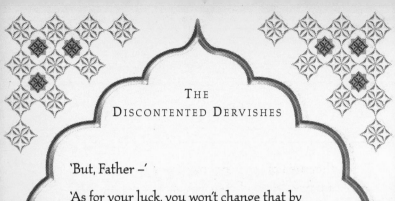

THE
DISCONTENTED DERVISHES

'But, Father –'

'As for your luck, you won't change that by force, you know. It's no use a bald man trying to dye his hair – and that's exactly what you are like without luck. It doesn't matter if you have two hundred accomplishments for every hair of your head, without luck you might just as well have none. You might bare a strong arm, it's useless if it's an unlucky arm. No, no –'

'But, Father, listen, what about the many advantages I shall get by travelling? It will enliven my mind. Think of the wonderful things I shall see, the strange things I shall hear. What pleasures will come from visiting new cities, new countries, making new friends –'

'My dear son – '

'I shall acquire dignity, rank, property, and above all, experience of the world. And here's another saying: Stay-at-home, you will never be a man: travel the world before you leave it for ever.'

'Yes, yes, my dear son, the pleasures and advantages of travel are countless, I agree, but

they are not for everybody. I would say there
are five classes of men equipped to enjoy
them. Now, sit down, be patient, and listen
while I tell you what they are:

'Firstly, there are merchants, who are rich and
powerful enough to own slaves, both male and
female, and plenty of clever and brave servants.
They can move daily from town to town and
spend each night in a different place, enjoy
every luxury and every moment of their
journey. Mountains, deserts, they are all the
same to them – wherever they pitch their tent,
there they are at their ease. But how different
for the poor man, uncomfortable even in his
home!

'Secondly, come scholars. Now, these are
welcome wherever they go because of their
pleasant conversation, their eloquence, their
learning. Their presence is like gold whose
value is known the world over. Alas, an
ignorant man, even if he be of noble birth,
which you are not . . . well, need I say more?'

'I appreciate that, Father, but – '

69

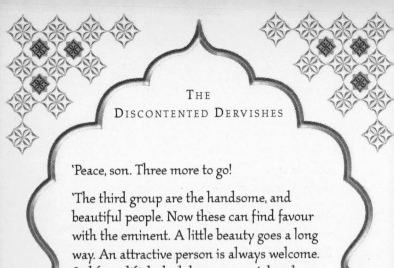

'Peace, son. Three more to go!

'The third group are the handsome, and beautiful people. Now these can find favour with the eminent. A little beauty goes a long way. An attractive person is always welcome. Sad faces lift, locked doors open. A handsome son . . . ah yes, a handsome son is like a pearl, which everyone wants to buy.

'As for the fourth group: these are the ones with sweet voices, those who like David can soothe the rages of kings, who can arrest birds in flight at the sound of their singing, who can capture the hearts of men, and enrapture the soulful. Yes, these are the ones who can travel, for all want to be their companions. How pleasant is a song in the morning! A delightful voice is even better than a handsome face, I think, for while the latter gladdens the senses, the former delights the soul.'

'And lastly, comes the workman. He can travel because he has a job at his fingertips. He needn't risk his name begging for bread. As the saying goes: A weaver can leave his home

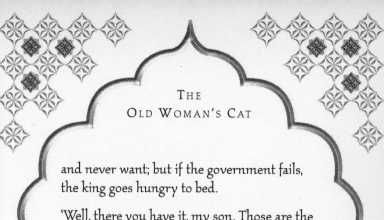

and never want; but if the government fails, the king goes hungry to bed.

'Well, there you have it, my son. Those are the people who can enjoy and benefit from travel. But if you do not have any of these qualities, and in all honesty ... yes, well, if you do not have them a hopeless journey lies before you, believe me. You will never be heard of again. You will be lost without trace. No, if affliction is your lot, accept your destiny.'

'Father,' said the youth, 'I've listened to all that. Now you tell me this: Isn't there a wise saying that, although food is allotted to each one of us, yet we still have to exert ourselves to get it? And another saying that calamity is decreed by fate. Why leave the door open to it? Everyone dies in the end: that's no reason to rush into a dragon's jaws.

'Look at me now. I'm strong. I could cope with a mad elephant, I could wrestle with a ravenous lion. Oh, I must travel! I can't put up with this misery any longer. I've no place here at all.

THE
DISCONTENTED DERVISHES

'Well, Father, what do you say? Do I have your blessing?'

The youth's father at last gave in and blessed his son.

'I will go where no one has ever heard of me,' said the youth. 'That's the best course for a clever man cursed with bad luck.' So he put on his best robe and set out on his journey.

Some time before he came to it, he could hear the sound of a river in full flood. When he arrived at the bank he saw the tremendous force of the water, sweeping boulders and heavy millstones in its dreadful headlong course. Even the birds, used to the river, sheltered, terrified, on the bank.

Then he saw that a ferryboat was preparing to cross. The passengers, with their baggage, were already on board.

'Is there room for me?' he called.

'There is,' replied the boatman, 'but for this crossing it will cost you one gold coin.'

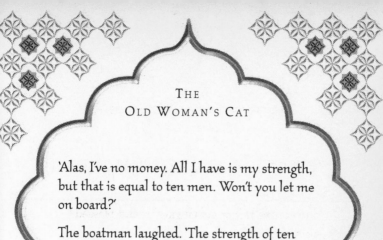

THE
OLD WOMAN'S CAT

'Alas, I've no money. All I have is my strength, but that is equal to ten men. Won't you let me on board?'

The boatman laughed. 'The strength of ten men will get you nowhere', he jeered. 'All you need is gold enough for one! Cast off there!'

The boat, with its laughing passengers, began its perilous journey.

'What about this robe I'm wearing?' the youth shouted. 'Would you be satisfied with that for payment?'

The boatman paused, and glanced back. It looked quite a good robe. He turned the boat round and brought it into the bank.

As soon as the youth could reach, he grabbed the boatman by the beard and knocked him down on to the ground where he lay winded. The assistant boatman, who came to his aid, got the same treatment. The youth then looked as if he might attack the passengers, such was his fury, but – 'Hold, hold!' they cried, 'we have no quarrel with you, kind sir.

Come aboard. Look, there's a seat.'

By this time the boatman had got up. They were smarting, and eager for revenge but the rest of the passengers wanted no more trouble. They persuaded the boatman to cast off and the crossing began in earnest.

It took all the boatman's strength to keep it on the course marked by a ruined Grecian pillar which stuck up in the middle of the river. The boat rocked up and down, swirled about by the currents and eddying waves. All the passengers cried out, fearing for their lives. It got worse as they drew near to the middle.

'We're in terrible danger!' the chief boatman cried. 'Is there one of you strong enough to leap on to that pillar with this rope, to secure us until the river subsides?'

'Yes, I'll do it!' cried the youth. He grabbed the rope, jumped, and landed on top of the pillar and pulled the boat in. And then, the boatman got his revenge. Suddenly, he snatched the rope, and pushed off the boat. He laughed heartily as he steered the boat for the opposite bank.

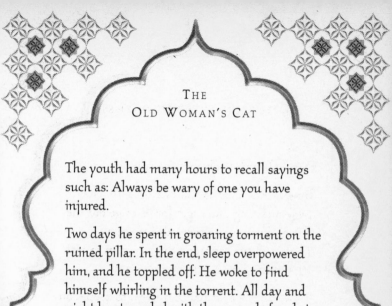

THE
OLD WOMAN'S CAT

The youth had many hours to recall sayings such as: Always be wary of one you have injured.

Two days he spent in groaning torment on the ruined pillar. In the end, sleep overpowered him, and he toppled off. He woke to find himself whirling in the torrent. All day and night he struggled with the waves before being cast, more dead than alive, on the bank.

Famished, he ate leaves and grass in desperation, until he gathered enough strength to make his way inland. There he suffered the torments of thirst in the desert.

As last he managed to reach a well. People were buying and drinking the water for as little as one pashizi. But, small and insignificant as this coin is, it was more than the youth possessed. And no one took pity on him. He began to insult them, then, but it made no difference, until, in his desperation, he attacked them, knocking down one or two men. They all turned on him and overpowered and beat him, before setting off on their journey.

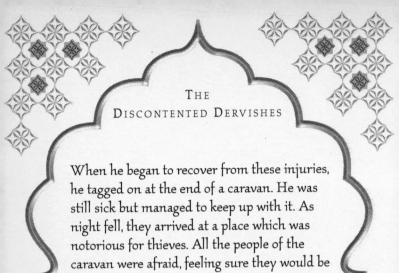

When he began to recover from these injuries, he tagged on at the end of a caravan. He was still sick but managed to keep up with it. As night fell, they arrived at a place which was notorious for thieves. All the people of the caravan were afraid, feeling sure they would be killed.

The youth seized his opportunity.

'Don't be afraid', he said. 'On my own I can cope with fifty men! And I'm sure that the youths among us can deal with any that are left.'

The boastful words cheered the travellers. They welcomed the youth and decided to supply him with food and water. He ate and drank ravenously, until his pangs subsided. Then, overcome with fatigue, he fell asleep.

Now, one of the travellers, who was old and experienced, seeing that the youth slept, spoke quietly to some of his fellow travellers.

'My friends', he said, 'I am minded of the story of the Arab who, having accumulated a small sum of money, could not sleep for fear that

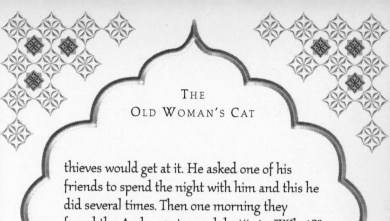

thieves would get at it. He asked one of his
friends to spend the night with him and this he
did several times. Then one morning they
found the Arab weeping and destitute. "What?"
they said, "Did a thief get your money in the
end?" "Not a thief, but my friend!" he lamented.
And it was true. The friend had discovered
where the money was, and made off with it!

'Now, my fellow travellers', continued the old
man, 'it seems to me that we ought to be more
afraid of the friend sleeping there than of the
thieves from whom he is supposed to be
protecting us. I think we ought to depart quietly,
and let him slumber on. What do you say?'

Long after the sun had risen, the youth woke
– to find himself alone and deserted. He
wandered about in a hopeless attempt to find
the way. Then, thirsty and in despair, he sank
down ready to die.

'The camels have moved on. Who will help me
now?' he groaned. 'The poor have no one to
befriend them except those who are poor
themselves.'

THE
DISCONTENTED DERVISHES

Now it happened that a prince, who was out hunting and had become separated from his party, overheard the words of the despairing youth. He saw that, even though he was in rags, the youth had a fine physique.

'How do you come to be here?' he asked. The youth poured out his story, and the prince took pity on him. When his party rejoined him, he gave the youth some rich robes and other gifts, and detailed a servant to accompany him.

So it was that the youth, richly dressed and attended by the servant bearing gifts, returned to his home town and was welcomed by his delighted father. That night he told the story of his journey, of the adventure of the boat and the boatman's trick, of his treatment at the well, and the treachery of the travellers.

'There!' said his father, 'what did I tell you? Did I not warn you, when you set out, that empty hands are like the broken claws of a lion?'

'O, Father!' the youth cried, 'how will you get treasure unless you endure pain? How

subdue a foe unless you risk your life? You
cannot reap unless you sow. Can't you see
that, just for a little trouble, I have brought
home all this treasure? For a few tiny stings I
have obtained all this honey. A diver afraid of
crocodiles will never bring up pearls. What
does a lion eat if he stays in his den? What
food does a fallen hawk obtain? How – '

'Enough! Enough!' interrupted the father. 'All
right, I agree. This time heaven has befriended
you. Good luck smiled on you in the shape of
a prince who took pity and mended your
broken fortunes. But this is pure coincidence!
You can't govern your life on rare events of
this sort. The hunter does not catch his prey
every time. One day a lion will get him. So
beware lest . . . are you listening? Let me tell
you this story, and then, I'm off to bed:

'There was once a king of Persia who had a
ring in which was embedded a costly jewel.
Once, to amuse his courtiers, he commanded
the ring should be suspended on the dome of
a mosque. He announced that whoever should
shoot an arrow through the ring could claim it

as his own. Four hundred archers attempted the feat. All failed.

'It happened that a boy was shooting off arrows in all directions from the roof of a nearby monastery. The morning breeze caught one of his arrows – and carried it neatly through the ring. The precious jewel was his. Not only this, but the King gave him a robe of honour and other gifts as well.

'They found the boy burning his bow and arrows. When they asked him why he did this, he replied:

'"I'll never surpass this glory, but I might be tempted to try."'

The Beast and its Burden

'NO ONE COULD BE IN greater distress than I,' wailed a man in the desert. He had been left behind by the caravan.

'What misfortune!' he cried. 'This is the end.'

'Be quiet,' said a donkey, passing with its owner on its back. 'If you have no beast to ride, at least you can be grateful that you're not a beast that's ridden upon!'

The Heart's Desire

A SICK MAN was asked:

'What does your heart desire?'

He replied: 'If only it would desire anything!'

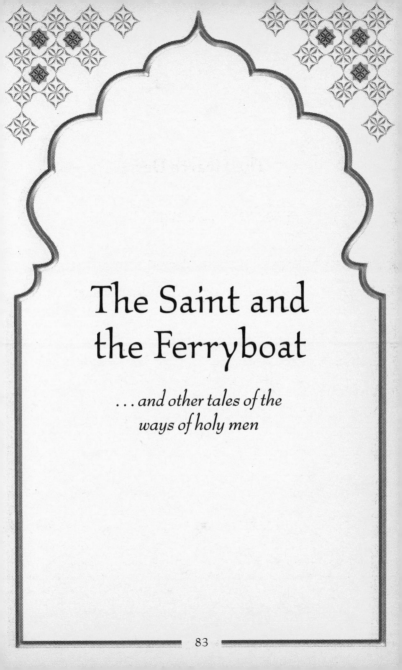

The Saint and the Ferryboat

*...and other tales of the
ways of holy men*

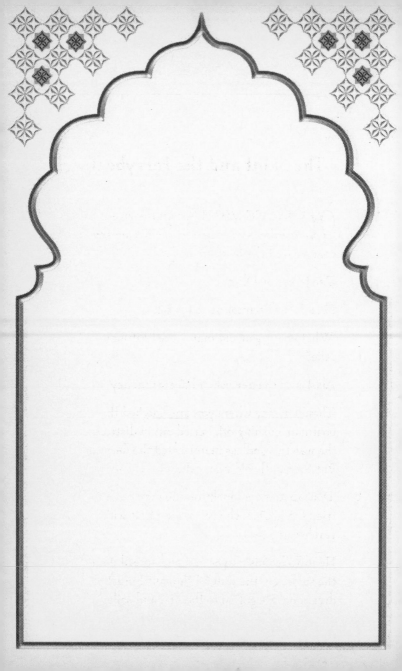

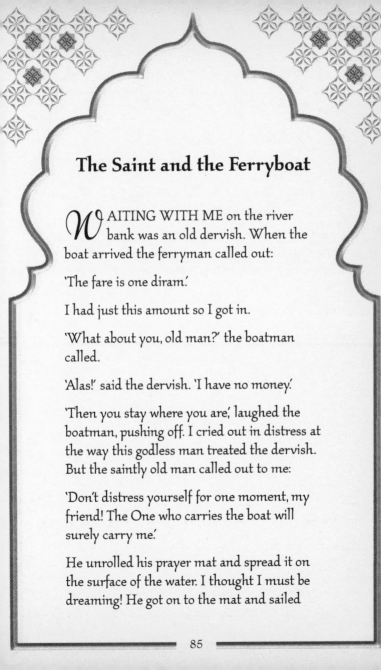

The Saint and the Ferryboat

*W*AITING WITH ME on the river bank was an old dervish. When the boat arrived the ferryman called out:

'The fare is one diram.'

I had just this amount so I got in.

'What about you, old man?' the boatman called.

'Alas!' said the dervish. 'I have no money.'

'Then you stay where you are,' laughed the boatman, pushing off. I cried out in distress at the way this godless man treated the dervish. But the saintly old man called out to me:

'Don't distress yourself for one moment, my friend! The One who carries the boat will surely carry me.'

He unrolled his prayer mat and spread it on the surface of the water. I thought I must be dreaming! He got on to the mat and sailed across the river – quite safely.

I was so amazed I couldn't sleep all night. In the morning the old man laughed at me.

'Still astonished?' he chuckled. 'It couldn't be simpler. The boat brought you and God brought me!'

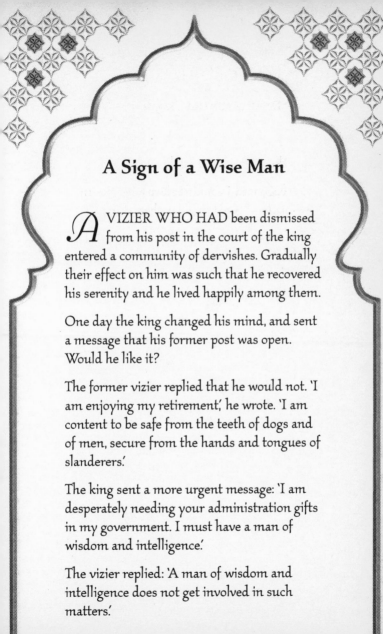

A Sign of a Wise Man

A VIZIER WHO HAD been dismissed from his post in the court of the king entered a community of dervishes. Gradually their effect on him was such that he recovered his serenity and he lived happily among them.

One day the king changed his mind, and sent a message that his former post was open. Would he like it?

The former vizier replied that he would not. 'I am enjoying my retirement', he wrote. 'I am content to be safe from the teeth of dogs and of men, secure from the hands and tongues of slanderers.'

The king sent a more urgent message: 'I am desperately needing your administration gifts in my government. I must have a man of wisdom and intelligence.'

The vizier replied: 'A man of wisdom and intelligence does not get involved in such matters.'

The Unsuccessful Thief

*O*NE NIGHT A THIEF broke into the house of a poor and holy hermit. He crept from room to room but could not find anything to steal. Sadly, he left the house.

But the hermit, who had been awake all the time, called down to the thief:

'I'm sorry you couldn't find anything. I can't bear to have you go away in despair. Take this.' And he threw down the blanket on which he had been sleeping.

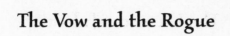

The Vow and the Rogue

'*I*F THIS IMPORTANT MATTER turns out as I want', vowed the king, 'then I will give this large purse of money to be distributed among all the holy men in this city'.

The important matter turned out exactly as he desired. The king called one of his favourite servants, gave him the fat purse and sent him out to distribute the contents.

The servant, so the story goes, was intelligent and shrewd. All day he went about the city and, as night fell, he returned to the palace. He kissed the purse, from which not one coin had been taken, and laid it at the feet of the king.

'I couldn't find any holy men', he said.

'Nonsense!' said the king. 'Why, I know for a fact that there are at least four hundred in the city'.

'King of the World', the servant replied, 'I knew that holy men never accept money; so those who were prepared to do so could not be holy men.'

The king laughed. 'This rogue doesn't like holy men and so he has thwarted my desire to help them,' he said to his courtiers. 'But I can't help feeling that he is right.'

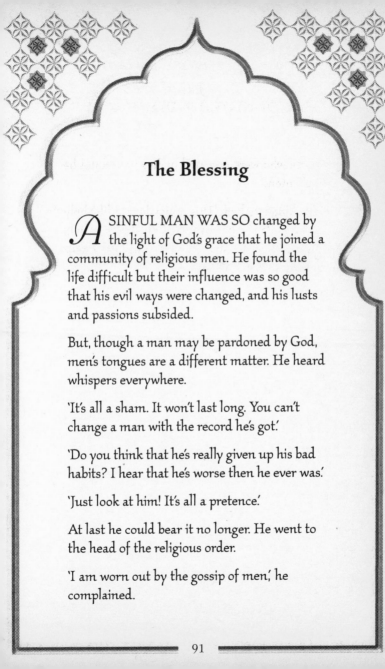

The Blessing

A SINFUL MAN WAS SO changed by
the light of God's grace that he joined a
community of religious men. He found the
life difficult but their influence was so good
that his evil ways were changed, and his lusts
and passions subsided.

But, though a man may be pardoned by God,
men's tongues are a different matter. He heard
whispers everywhere.

'It's all a sham. It won't last long. You can't
change a man with the record he's got.'

'Do you think that he's really given up his bad
habits? I hear that he's worse then he ever was.'

'Just look at him! It's all a pretence.'

At last he could bear it no longer. He went to
the head of the religious order.

'I am worn out by the gossip of men,' he
complained.

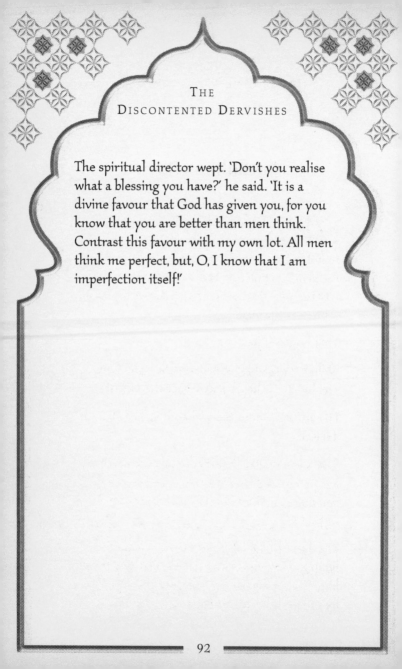

THE
DISCONTENTED DERVISHES

The spiritual director wept. 'Don't you realise what a blessing you have?' he said. 'It is a divine favour that God has given you, for you know that you are better than men think. Contrast this favour with my own lot. All men think me perfect, but, O, I know that I am imperfection itself!'

The Sultan's Boon

A SOLITARY DERVISH found happiness and peace, sitting in a remote part of the desert. One day, the sultan happened to journey that way, but the dervish was so lost in his contentment that he did not even raise his head.

This angered the sultan.

'What a ragged lot of beggars these dervishes are,' he said. 'They are no better than beasts!'

His vizier dismounted and approached the dervish.

'Don't you realise that the king of the earth has just passed?' he said. 'He wonders why you do not do him homage? Where is your respect?'

The dervish said: 'Tell the sultan to expect homage from those who need something from him. If I am ragged and a beggar, then it is for him to protect me. If I am a beast, let him

remember that the shepherd is there to serve the sheep, not the other way round. And Fate makes nonsense of the difference between sultans and beggars. Open any tomb: what distinguishes a rich man from a poor one?'

In spite of himself, the sultan was impressed by what the dervish said. He went up to him.

'Have you any special advice for me?' he asked.

'Only this: you are rich now, but don't forget that your wealth, your land, your entire kingdom will one day leave your hand and go to another's.'

'Thank you. Is there any boon that I can grant you?'

'Yes,' said the dervish. 'Please don't disturb me again.'

The Pious Man's Reward

A PIOUS MAN ONCE dreamed that he saw a king in Paradise and a pious man in Hell.

'That's not right', he exclaimed. 'Surely it should be the other way round?'

'Not at all', came the answer. 'The king is in Heaven because he loved and befriended dervishes; the pious man is in Hell because he associated too much with kings'.

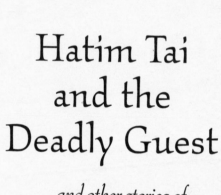

Hatim Tai
and the
Deadly Guest

*...and other stories of
the generous, the mean,
the wise and the foolish*

Hatim Tai and the Deadly Guest

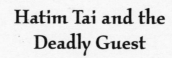

*T*HE KING WAS ALWAYS wondering what his people *really* thought about him.

So, one day, he disguised himself as a beggar. He went into the market-place, and discovered that his people weren't thinking about him at all!

They were full of praise for a chieftain, who lived far away, called Hatim Tai.

'Have you heard the latest tale of his generosity?' said a merchant. 'They say that . . .'

'That is nothing! What about his marvellous horse? Did you hear that . . .'

'And his courage . . .'

'. . . his wisdom.'

The king returned in a bad temper.

THE
DISCONTENTED DERVISHES

'Noble! Generous! Courageous! They should be saying that about *me*, their king,' he muttered angrily. He sent for his special servant, Farid. Farid was tall, always dressed in black; his thin face was pale, his eyes cold.

'You have heard of this Hatim Tai?' the king demanded.

'Who has not, my lord?'

'I shall not rest until he is dead. I want you to kill him,' ordered the king. 'Bring me his head.'

Farid was startled.

'Well?' the king shouted.

'It shall be done,' muttered Farid, and his strong hand clasped his sword.

That night, a black shadow left the palace, and journeyed into day, after day, after weary day. Farid searched the far reaches of the kingdom for Hatim Tai. He could not be found.

'Can you tell me of Hatim?' he called from his horse to the people he met. They looked at his sword, at his face, and into his eyes. They

100

shuddered, shook their heads, and left. No one would give him shelter.

After many nights and days of travelling, Farid was exhausted. He rested in the oasis. The desert was before him. He fell asleep.

Towards evening, he woke suddenly. A young man sat there. Farid's hand flew to his sword.

'Do not be alarmed,' said the man. 'Do you journey far?'

'I have travelled many days and nights,' said Farid.

'Then you do well to rest. You are nobly born, I see. Perhaps you are on an urgent mission for your lord. Do you care to eat and stay the night with me . . .?'

Farid agreed. He followed the young man to a group of tents. Water was provided to wash him, and clean robes were brought. The gong sounded. Farid was welcomed into another tent where food was laid out. Smiling servants waited on Farid and the young man.

'I am not rich, but everything I have is yours,'
said the young man. He was so friendly, so
eager to make him welcome, that Farid felt the
tiredness leave him.

They talked into the night, of many things.
'But you must sleep,' said the young man. He
summoned servants and Farid was shown
into a quiet tent. He slept peacefully.

The next morning, the young man begged
Farid to stay.

Farid said: 'I should like to, for I would know
more of you. But I am on a secret mission. I
feel I can trust you. I search for a chieftain
called Hatim Tai. Do you know where he is?
The king wants his life, and he has sent me to
kill him.'

'If the king seeks Hatim's life, it must be for a
good reason,' said the young man, sadly. 'And
you,' he continued, 'what will the king do to
you if you fail to do his bidding?'

Farid smiled bitterly. 'Assuredly, the king will
take my own life,' he said.

The young man nodded. 'My way is clear,' he said. 'O noble Farid, you are my guest and therefore my friend. I would not have a friend in danger of his life for my sake. Take out your sword.'

The young man knelt before the astonished Farid. 'I am Hatim Tai, the man you seek. Strike off my head, satisfy the king, and save your life.'

Shocked, Farid the killer, drew his sword, and threw it away from him. 'Let my sword lie forever in the desert!' he cried. 'If I harm one hair of your noble head I should no longer be Farid the man, but a dog without a name. Rise, Hatim, and let me kneel before *you*, then let me embrace you and make you forever a friend.'

The king rejoiced to see Farid's return.

'Is Hatim Tai dead?' he demanded, puzzled. Farid's hands were empty, he was without his sword, and now he had thrown himself prostrate before the throne.

THE
DISCONTENTED DERVISHES

'O wise and just king!' said Farid. 'After many days' search, Hatim revealed himself to me. I found that he, too, is wise and just, generous and of a true and noble mind – with a courage greater than my own. He slew all that was evil in me with the sword of his love!'

It is said that when Farid told all, the king lost his anger, and was ashamed. He rewarded Farid with much gold and sent to ask Hatim to visit him.

And when Hatim Tai came, the king wept, then rejoiced and embraced him.

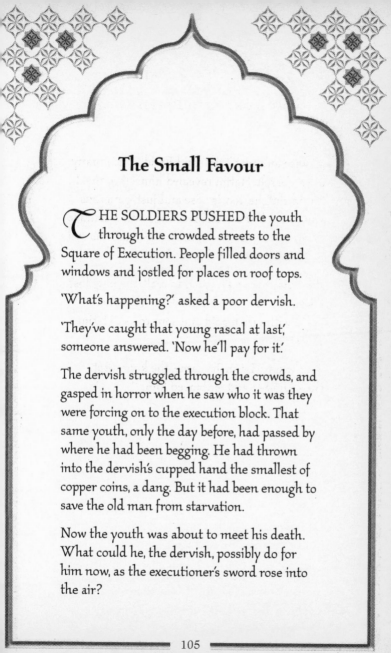

The Small Favour

THE SOLDIERS PUSHED the youth through the crowded streets to the Square of Execution. People filled doors and windows and jostled for places on roof tops.

'What's happening?' asked a poor dervish.

'They've caught that young rascal at last,' someone answered. 'Now he'll pay for it.'

The dervish struggled through the crowds, and gasped in horror when he saw who it was they were forcing on to the execution block. That same youth, only the day before, had passed by where he had been begging. He had thrown into the dervish's cupped hand the smallest of copper coins, a dang. But it had been enough to save the old man from starvation.

Now the youth was about to meet his death. What could he, the dervish, possibly do for him now, as the executioner's sword rose into the air?

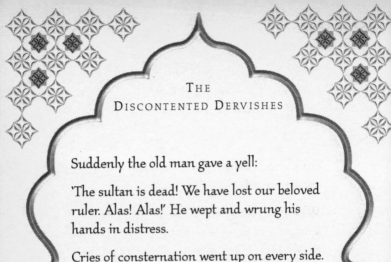

Suddenly the old man gave a yell:

'The sultan is dead! We have lost our beloved ruler. Alas! Alas!' He wept and wrung his hands in distress.

Cries of consternation went up on every side. People sobbed, beating their heads and breasts. The soldiers ran to the palace. The crowd followed – everyone, that is, except the youth. They forgot about him and he slipped from their midst and made off.

The soldiers burst into the palace and into the throne room. There, on the throne, very much alive, sat the puzzled sultan.

They soon caught the old man and dragged him before the throne.

'What did you mean by this?' demanded the sultan. 'Am I not a good and upright ruler? What possessed you then to desire my death and cause all this distress?'

'Great and powerful king', replied the dervish, 'it was, I admit, a false word that I uttered, but not only are you not dead, to

our obvious delight, but a helpless one escaped death as well.'

When the sultan heard the full story, he was amused and delighted with the cleverness of the dervish. He gave him a gift and said no more.

As for the youth, stumbling his way out of the city, he was hailed by someone who asked:

'How did you escape death?'

'Through an old man's courage – oh, and a dang!' he replied.

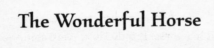

The Wonderful Horse

'TELL ME ABOUT THIS famous horse of Hatim Tai's,' ordered the sultan. He was tired of overhearing whispers and rumours, and of having his own horses compared unfavourably with this renowned steed of the Arabian chieftain.

The sultan's courtiers were only too eager to satisfy him.

'It is the colour of smoke,' said one.

'As swift as the dawn breeze,' said another.

'No, no, swifter,' said a third, 'for it leaves the wind behind in the dust.'

'It flies faster than a bird!'

'It's neighing is like thunder!'

'If flashes by like lightning!'

The sultan listened patiently. 'Well, well,' he said, 'it seems to me that just as there is no one in the world more generous than Hatim

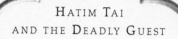

HATIM TAI
AND THE DEADLY GUEST

Tai, so now there is no horse in the world to
match his horse. If only there were some way
of measuring the truth, not only about the
horse, but of his generosity as well.'

He discussed this with his vizier. At length,
'I have it!' said the sultan, 'and it is so simple
that I must be inspired! I will send and ask
Hatim Tai to give me the horse!'

'Your majesty?'

'Don't you see?' he cried. 'Hatim Tai has this
reputation for being generous. Well, here is a
supreme way of testing it – and also of
acquiring that horse.'

'But if he refuses?'

'If he refuses, where is his famous generosity?
I shall have shown the world that his
reputation is as the noise of an empty drum.
Well, what do you think?'

'An excellent scheme, your majesty.'

'Of course it is. And who, but yourself, is
equipped with the skill and tact to carry it

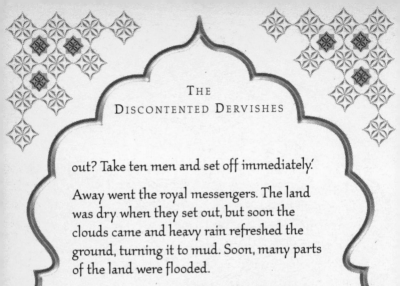

out? Take ten men and set off immediately.'

Away went the royal messengers. The land
was dry when they set out, but soon the
clouds came and heavy rain refreshed the
ground, turning it to mud. Soon, many parts
of the land were flooded.

When at last, the wet and weary travellers
arrived, Hatim Tai himself came out to bid
them welcome. They were shown to prepared
rooms, given fresh clothes, and invited to
a feast.

All were astonished at the splendour of the
meal. The roast meat was succulent; there
were rich, sweet dishes to follow; the cups
were of gold.

'And now,' said Hatim Tai, when all were
satisfied, 'what can I do for the sultan?'

Delicately, the vizier began to reveal the
purpose of his mission. But, as he continued,
he saw a cloud of sadness cross Hatim Tai's
face. And when he spoke of the sultan's
request, Hatim Tai cried out in distress.

'Oh, my friend, why didn't you tell me this before? When you all arrived I was at a loss, for the floods have made it impossible at the moment to reach my cattle. One animal only was at my gates, the famed horse of which you spoke. I killed it and had it roasted. I could not let you go to bed hungry, even if I never find another steed like this one.'

Several days later, the envoys returned to the sultan, bearing gifts of gold, rich robes, and horses. When he heard their story he could not help but applaud the generosity of Hatim Tai.

When The Idol Didn't Answer

A MAN ONCE GAVE himself up to the worship of an idol. For several years all went well, then some problem occurred that he could not solve. He rolled in the dust in the temple before the idol, weeping: 'Help me, Idol. I'm about to die. O pity me.'

He prayed and begged like this for a long time. But there was no response.

At last the man cried:

'O, Idol! I must have been shackled in error all the years I have worshipped you! Help me now in this calamity or I will turn to the Almighty and ask him to help me.' Still there was no response.

He left the temple and had not time to clean the dust from his face before the Almighty granted his wish.

A wise man, who observed all this, was astonished.

'What?' he said to himself, 'a mean worshipper of an idol, unfaithful and false – yet God gave him what he wanted!' He could not understand it until God sent a message to his heart:

'It is true that the foolish old man spent many years worshipping the idol. He asked for help but his prayer was rejected. But if I reject him too, what difference is there between me and the idol?'

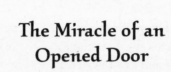

The Miracle of an Opened Door

*C*HE POOR DERVISH sat down in the dust and wept. A blind man heard the cries and groped towards him.

'What is the matter?' he asked.

'I had hoped for help from the proud rich man who lives here,' replied the dervish in angry despair. 'But he has just shut the door in my face.'

'Don't cry a moment longer,' said the blind man. He reached out and touched the dervish and tugged at the collar of his robe. 'Come to my place,' he said, pulling the dervish to his feet. 'Come and eat with me. Stay the night.'

When they arrived at the blind man's lodging, he prepared a meal and laid it before the dervish. When they had eaten, the grateful dervish prayed:

'May God grant you your sight!'

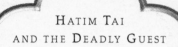

In the night, the blind man felt tears trickle down his cheek. In the morning he opened his eyes – and saw the world!

News of the miracle spread all over the city. Even the proud rich man was interested and sought the former blind man out.

'Tell me how it happened', he begged. 'Who was it who brought light into your dark world?'

'O foolish tyrant, and blind of heart', replied the man. 'Do you recall the dervish who cried at your house? If you would have light in your dark heart, kiss the dust at the feet of such men. Last night you shut your door in the face of the dervish. It was that same dervish who opened the door in mine.'

The Miser and His Son

*T*HERE WAS A MAN who had much gold but was unable to enjoy it. Food cost money, so he ate very little. Beggars got nothing out of him – he was saving for Judgment Day! Night and day his mind was chained by the thoughts of his gold and silver.

Where did he keep all his gold? This was what his son wanted to know, so he watched closely and followed him secretly. At last he discovered the spot. His father was hiding the money in the ground.

In no time the son had dug the caskets up. He removed the gold and filled the caskets with stones. Off he went on a wild spending spree. He took out the gold with one hand and spent it with the other. It didn't last long in the bazaars and gambling dens.

You should have heard the cries of the old miser when he discovered his loss. He wept and wailed all night. As for the son, he too was up all night, playing on his flute and harp!

In the morning the son went in to his anguished parent. 'On Father,' he laughed, 'gold is for enjoying! If all you can do with it is bury it in the earth, stones will do just as well.'

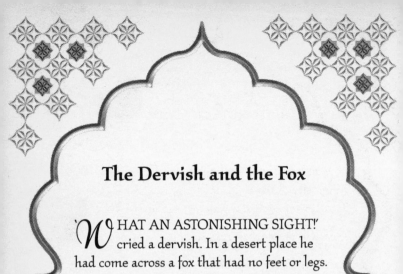

The Dervish and the Fox

'*W*HAT AN ASTONISHING SIGHT!'
cried a dervish. In a desert place he
had come across a fox that had no feet or legs.

'How can it possibly live?' he wondered, 'for it
looks healthy enough.'

Then he jumped behind a rock in terror. A
lion had come upon the scene.

The lion had killed a jackal. It dropped the
carcase near the fox, ate its fill, and then went
off, leaving bits of the meat behind. Quickly
the fox ate the lot.

'Even more astonishing!' gasped the dervish.
He couldn't believe what he had seen so next
day he came out into the desert and again hid
behind the rock. The same thing happened.
The lion appeared with a freshly killed jackal,
ate what it wanted, leaving portions of the
meat for the fox to finish.

'It's a sign from God!' the dervish said. 'From

now on I, too, will rely, like the fox, upon the generosity of the Creator. He found himself a dark corner against a wall and settled to wait.

'God will provide,' he said to himself.

He sat there for several days and neither friend nor stranger went near him. More days passed. He grew thinner and thinner until his veins and skin were stretched like harp strings on his bony frame.

At length, when he was almost too weak to move, a holy man stood before him and enquired what was the matter.

The dervish poured out his story. 'Now tell me,' he said when he had finished, 'surely that was a sign from God?'

'Of course it was,' replied the holy man, 'but how could you be such an idiot? Why didn't you see that you were supposed to imitate not the fox but the lion?'

The Smooth Talker

A SMOOTH-TALKING rascal stopped a good-hearted man one day and poured out his problem.

'I'm so deeply stuck in the mire,' he said, 'that I'll never get out. I owe ten dirams to a man so mean and troublesome that even the smallest coin in that sum is a heavy burden on my heart. I can't get to sleep at night for worrying about it. Every morning without fail, he knocks at my door, and for the rest of the day he follows me about like a shadow, wounding me with the most distressing insults. It's as if he had no other money in the world. I'm sure that the only chapter in the Book of Religion that he's read is the one that says: Don't spend. I'm at my wit's end. If only some kind people would help me out with a coin or two.'

The kind man listened to this tale with obvious sympathy and gave him two gold coins. The fellow went on his way with a face shining like the sun.

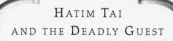

An astonished friend said to the kind-hearted man. 'Surely you have come across this character before? He's well known in these parts. If he died tomorrow not a soul would mourn him. He's such a crafty and deceitful beggar that he could saddle a tiger!'

'Enough!' the generous man replied. 'The way I look at it is this: Either he was telling the truth, in which case I have saved his honour; or he was lying, in which case I have protected mine. Even a blameless man's honour needs protecting from a man as devious and talkative as that.'

A Rope with a Name

I SAW A BOY COMING towards me with a sheep running after him.

'No wonder the sheep follows you so closely,' I remarked, 'attached to you as it is by that rope round its neck.'

The boy laughed and released the animal. Off it went, gambolling in delight.

Then the boy made to move on. Immediately the sheep came to his heel and followed close behind.

The youth smiled and gave it some barley.

'You were right, wise man,' he said, ' but, as you see, the name of the rope is kindness.'

Rich Man, Poor Man

A WEAK AND STARVING dervish once begged at the door of a rich man.

'Away with you', said the wealthy man in proud anger, 'you'll get nothing from me!'

How the dervish's heart bled at this. 'It is astonishing that such a man should be so severe', he said. 'It is obvious that he has had no experience of begging.'

'Is he gone?' shouted the rich man to his slave. 'If not, go and clear him from my door.' The slave came out and drove the dervish away.

Now I heard that, because he was not truly grateful to the One who provides all, circumstances changed soon after for that rich man. His fortunes altered dramatically and suddenly he was ruined. He was not left even with an ass upon which to carry away his personal belongings – which was perhaps as well because he hadn't any.

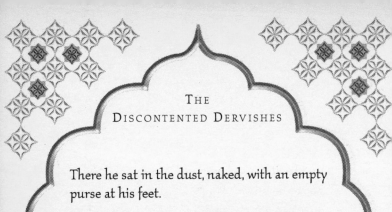

There he sat in the dust, naked, with an empty purse at his feet.

The slave was sold to another master. The new master was also rich but there the similarity to his old master ended, for this one was kind and generous to all, rich in goods and in heart. When he saw a poor man, he rejoiced at the opportunity to be generous. He was as delighted to give as the poor man was to receive.

One night he heard a cry at his door.

'A morsel! Please, I beg, one morsel!'

'Slave', said the kind man, 'take the tray from the table. Go and gladden that beggar's heart.'

The slave did as he was ordered. He returned with tears flooding down his cheeks.

'What is the matter?' the master asked.

'It is the beggar', the slave cried. 'I have just recognised him. He was my old master. He once owned vast property, silver and gold. But now, look at him, a destitute beggar.'

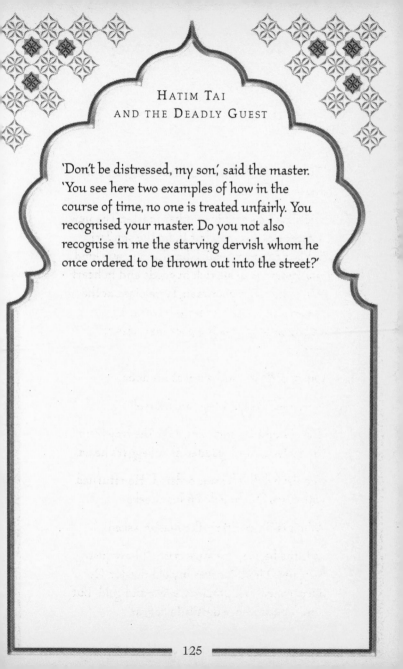

HATIM TAI
AND THE DEADLY GUEST

'Don't be distressed, my son,' said the master.
'You see here two examples of how in the
course of time, no one is treated unfairly. You
recognised your master. Do you not also
recognise in me the starving dervish whom he
once ordered to be thrown out into the street?'

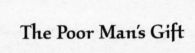

The Poor Man's Gift

*T*HERE WAS A KIND and good man who never had enough money to be as generous to others as he wanted to be. As soon as he had any money, he gave it away, so he was always poor.

One day a message was brought to him from the prison:

'Please help me,' the letter said, 'for I have heard much of your generous nature. I have been in prison here for many days, all because of a debt of a few dirams.'

The amount, though small, was more than the good man had. He therefore sent a message to the prisoner's creditors.

'Noble sirs, I pray you let this debtor out for a bit. I will stand security for him should he escape.'

This was agreed and a sum of silver was fixed as security. Then the good man visited the prisoner.

'When they let you out, run for it,' he said.

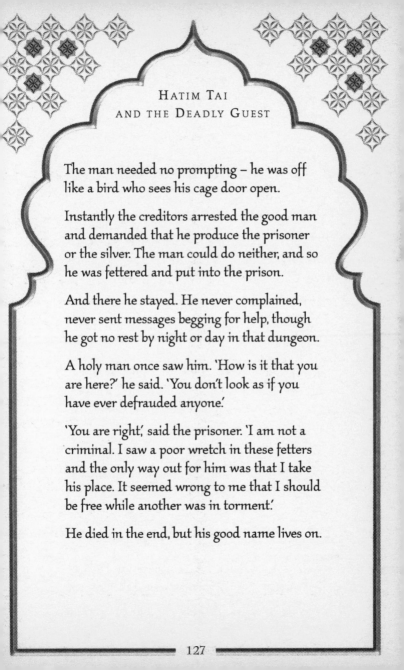

HATIM TAI
AND THE DEADLY GUEST

The man needed no prompting – he was off like a bird who sees his cage door open.

Instantly the creditors arrested the good man and demanded that he produce the prisoner or the silver. The man could do neither, and so he was fettered and put into the prison.

And there he stayed. He never complained, never sent messages begging for help, though he got no rest by night or day in that dungeon.

A holy man once saw him. 'How is it that you are here?' he said. 'You don't look as if you have ever defrauded anyone.'

'You are right', said the prisoner. 'I am not a criminal. I saw a poor wretch in these fetters and the only way out for him was that I take his place. It seemed wrong to me that I should be free while another was in torment.'

He died in the end, but his good name lives on.

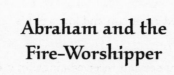

Abraham and the
Fire-Worshipper

*I*T WAS THE CUSTOM of Abraham to invite all needy travellers who passed to stay and eat at his house. Indeed, it was usual for him to go without a meal in the morning unless he had such a guest to share it.

I hear that, once, a whole week passed and not one traveller called. Abraham went out and looked up and down the road. There was no one in sight. He glanced across the valley. And there, in the distance, he saw a figure.

When Abraham drew nearer he found a little old man, with white hair, bent and solitary, like a lonely willow tree. After they had exchanged greetings, Abraham said:

'Old man, you would be doing me a favour if you would consent to come and share a meal with me in my house.'

'With pleasure!' cried the old man, who had

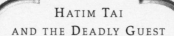

recognised Abraham and knew of his
generosity.

Abraham's servant received him with great
respect and courtesy. When all were seated
the meal was brought in.

Before they ate, the usual prayer was said, but
Abraham noticed that his guest did not join
in. He could not help but comment.

'I am surprised,' he said, 'not to find in you
the warm faith usual in a man of ripe years.
Before you eat, isn't it your custom to say a
payer to the Giver of all Food?'

'Why no,' admitted the old man. 'I was not
taught this by the priests who instructed me. I
am by religion a Fire-worshipper.'

Abraham was horrified. He had made himself
unclean, according to the law, by sitting at table
with a non-believer. He called the servants and
had the old man shown to the door.

It is said that at that moment an angel came
down from God with this message for
Abraham:

'Friend of God, it is true that he is a Fire-worshipper, but why did you turn him away? For a hundred years I have given life and food to him. Could you not entertain him for one meal?'

The Peacock

*I*T WAS A BEAUTIFUL BIRD. It spread its tail and astonished everyone with dazzling colours – everyone, that is, except a man of ill-will.

'What big ugly feet the bird has', he said.

The Good Deed

A VILLAGE CHIEF saw a man take a thorn out of the foot of an orphan. That night he dreamed of the man, sauntering with pleasure in the gardens of Paradise and saying:

'Look how many roses blossomed from that thorn!'

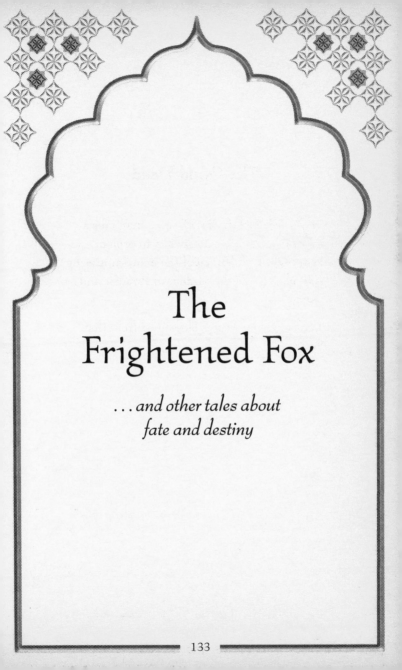

The Frightened Fox

...and other tales about fate and destiny

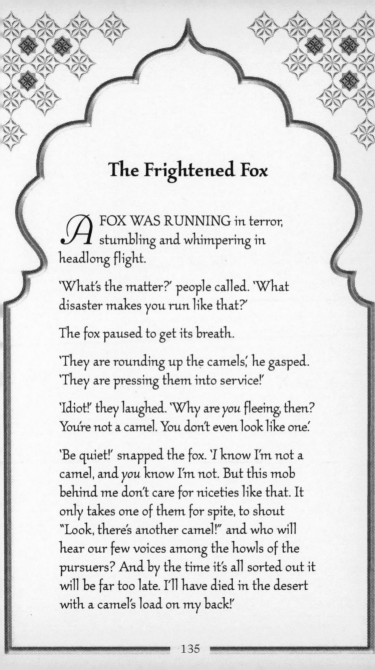

The Frightened Fox

A FOX WAS RUNNING in terror, stumbling and whimpering in headlong flight.

'What's the matter?' people called. 'What disaster makes you run like that?'

The fox paused to get its breath.

'They are rounding up the camels,' he gasped. 'They are pressing them into service!'

'Idiot!' they laughed. 'Why are *you* fleeing, then? You're not a camel. You don't even look like one.'

'Be quiet!' snapped the fox. 'I know I'm not a camel, and *you* know I'm not. But this mob behind me don't care for niceties like that. It only takes one of them for spite, to shout "Look, there's another camel!" and who will hear our few voices among the howls of the pursuers? And by the time it's all sorted out it will be far too late. I'll have died in the desert with a camel's load on my back!'

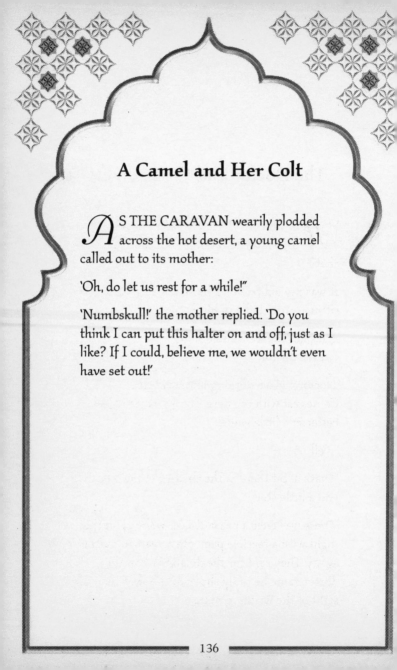

A Camel and Her Colt

*A*S THE CARAVAN wearily plodded across the hot desert, a young camel called out to its mother:

'Oh, do let us rest for a while!'"

'Numbskull!' the mother replied. 'Do you think I can put this halter on and off, just as I like? If I could, believe me, we wouldn't even have set out!'

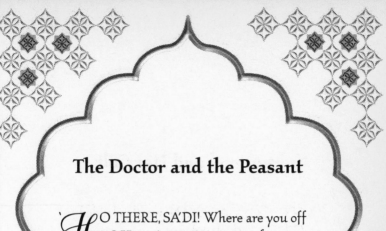

The Doctor and the Peasant

'*H*O THERE, SA'DI! Where are you off to? Haven't you time to stop for a chat?'

It was my old friend, a hero of many wars, sitting contentedly in his doorway.

'I am not too well', I told him. 'I am seeking out the doctor.'

'Doctors! Have nothing to do with them. Come rest with me here. See if you don't feel better in a little while.'

'Well . . .'

'That's it. Sit there in the shade. Let me tell you a little story:

'There was once a peasant who woke up in the night with a terrible pain. He screamed out in agony. They sent for the doctor. When the doctor came he sadly shook his head at the sight of the writhing man.

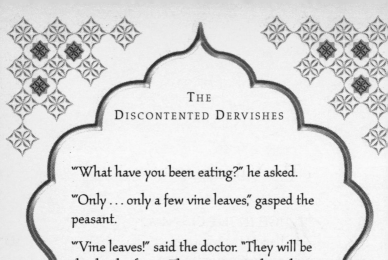

THE
DISCONTENTED DERVISHES

"'What have you been eating?' he asked.

"'Only . . . only a few vine leaves,' gasped the peasant.

"'Vine leaves!' said the doctor. 'They will be the death of you. They are worse than the Tartar's poisoned arrow. Prepare yourself. You won't last the night.'"

My old friend threw back his head and laughed.

'What happened?' I asked.

'Well, by chance – pure coincidence of course – the doctor himself died in the night!'

'And the peasant – what of him?'

The old solider laugher even louder.

'As you see, my dear Sa'di', he roared with tears coursing down his cheeks, 'as you see, I survived. All this took place well over forty years ago!'

The Vulture and the Kite

*H*IGH IN THE CLEAR AIR, two birds flew in the wind. One of the birds was a vulture. He hung in the air like a still, black flag.

The other bird was a kite. She soared and dipped and wheeled in the wind.

'What a marvellous day!' she cried. 'Don't you think so, vulture, my friend?'

'Be still,' snapped the vulture. 'We superior birds prefer to hover in the air, not flutter about like moths. How else can you look at the land below?'

'But I can see what is below,' answered the kite. 'My eyes are as good as yours.'

'That's nonsense!' sneered the vulture. 'Tell me what you can see.'

'I see the city,' the kite said.

'I should hope so!' scoffed the vulture. 'But I

can see, lurking in the shadow of a house in one of the streets, a skinny dog. Can you?'

The kite tried to see it.

'Let's go closer,' suggested the vulture. They flew down, wheeled and hovered, until the vulture hung still over a narrow street. There was the dog, its bright eyes looking up at them.

'You were right,' said the kite.

'Of course I was.'

The kite lifted away, soared high. The vulture, flapping slow black wings, followed.

'But if I look beyond the city,' shrieked the kite, 'I can see the distant hills, the streams, the trees, and a field where the grass moves like the sea.'

'Ah yes,' smiled the vulture, 'but my keener sight can pick out – there! – a bright-eyed mouse. You don't believe me? Let me show you.'

Again they swooped, and hung over the field. The mouse was still, terrified, but they detected it.

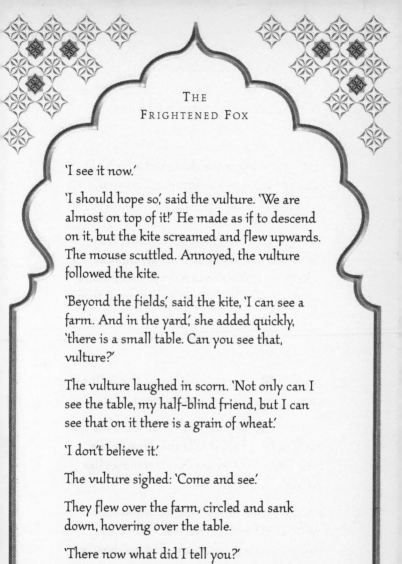

THE
FRIGHTENED FOX

'I see it now.'

'I should hope so,' said the vulture. 'We are almost on top of it!' He made as if to descend on it, but the kite screamed and flew upwards. The mouse scuttled. Annoyed, the vulture followed the kite.

'Beyond the fields,' said the kite, 'I can see a farm. And in the yard,' she added quickly, 'there is a small table. Can you see that, vulture?'

The vulture laughed in scorn. 'Not only can I see the table, my half-blind friend, but I can see that on it there is a grain of wheat.'

'I don't believe it.'

The vulture sighed: 'Come and see.'

They flew over the farm, circled and sank down, hovering over the table.

'There now what did I tell you?'

'You were right again,' said the kite, 'but now that we are closer, of course you can see that –'

'I can also show you,' interrupted the vulture proudly, 'that as well as having the best eyes of any bird, I can swoop and swirl like a kite, when the time comes. Watch me pluck up that grain of wheat.'

The kite screamed in alarm, but the vulture swooped, landed on the table, and caught up the grain of wheat. Suddenly – TWANG! – a wire writhed, tightened and caught hold.

'I'm caught, I'm caught!' screamed the vulture. 'It was a trap!'

He tried to fly up, but the man laughed as he came out of the bush, pulling on the wire, pulling and catching hold, dodging the swirling of wings, twisting the legs expertly. The vulture suddenly found himself in a cage.

The kite fluttered helplessly above as the vulture was taken away.

'What is the use of having the keenest eyes of all the birds if you can't see a trap?' she thought sadly as she floated freely in the wind.

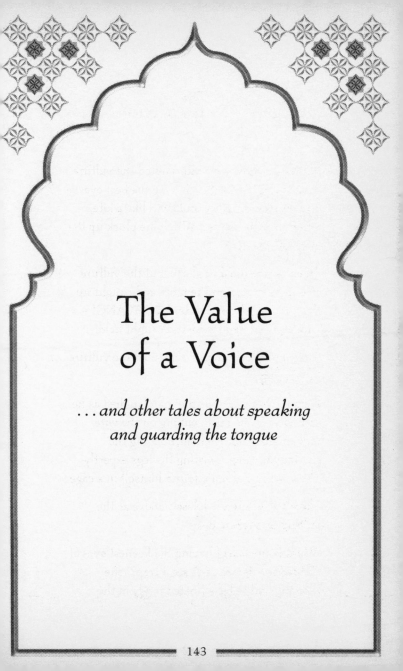

The Value
of a Voice

*...and other tales about speaking
and guarding the tongue*

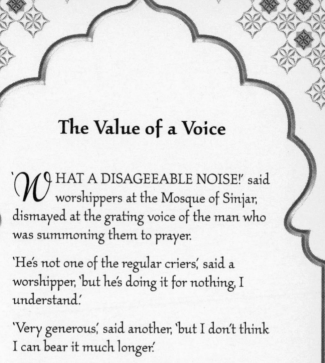

The Value of a Voice

'*WHAT A DISAGEEABLE NOISE!*' said worshippers at the Mosque of Sinjar, dismayed at the grating voice of the man who was summoning them to prayer.

'He's not one of the regular criers,' said a worshipper, 'but he's doing it for nothing, I understand.'

'Very generous,' said another, 'but I don't think I can bear it much longer.'

All this came to the ears of the owner of the Mosque. He was a kind and just prince, and while he knew he must do something, he did not want to give offence to the crier. He approached the man.

'My friend,' he said, 'thank you for what you are doing. However, as you may know, I do have a team of venerable and respected criers who have long summoned worshippers at the usual appointed hours. The job is passed down through their families from father to son, and

I give them an allowance of five dinars. Now, suppose I offered you ten dinars to move to another place?'

'I would accept it at once, my lord,' said the man. So an agreement was signed and off he went, to everyone's relief.

But, not long after, he returned to the prince.

'You did me an injustice, my lord,' he said, 'in sending me off from here for ten dinars. At the place where I am now they have just offered me twenty dinars to go away. However, I'm not going to accept it.'

'Quite right,' laughed the Prince. 'Don't you accept it. Believe me, before long, they will be offering you fifty!'

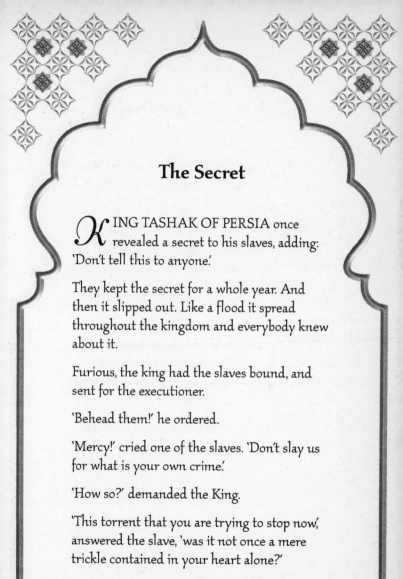

The Secret

KING TASHAK OF PERSIA once revealed a secret to his slaves, adding: 'Don't tell this to anyone.'

They kept the secret for a whole year. And then it slipped out. Like a flood it spread throughout the kingdom and everybody knew about it.

Furious, the king had the slaves bound, and sent for the executioner.

'Behead them!' he ordered.

'Mercy!' cried one of the slaves. 'Don't slay us for what is your own crime.'

'How so?' demanded the King.

'This torrent that you are trying to stop now,' answered the slave, 'was it not once a mere trickle contained in your heart alone?'

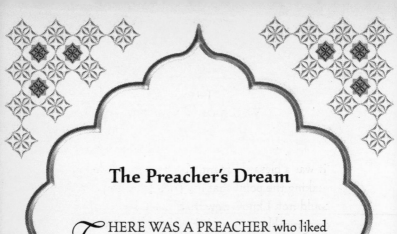

The Preacher's Dream

T HERE WAS A PREACHER who liked to think he had a beautiful and pleasing voice. In fact he sounded like a croaking raven. However, out of respect for him and his position, no one ever criticised him. They put up with his loud harshness, but squirmed inwardly.

But one day, another preacher in the area, who had a secret spite towards him, came on a visit.

'I've been dreaming about you', he said. 'I hope everything will turn out all right.'

'Good heavens! What did you dream?'

'O, don't get alarmed. I merely dreamed that your voice had suddenly become pleasant, and that people were comfortable when they heard you speak.'

The preacher was taken aback. He thought for a time, then he said:

THE
VALUE OF A VOICE

'It was a blessed dream. You have succeeded in making the point that my friends obviously could not. I know now that I have a disagreeable voice and that those who listen to me are far from happy with my speaking. Thank you, I will try to speak quietly and more agreeably in future.'

Why I am Prime Minister

*S*OME OF THE SERVANTS of Sultan Mahmud, curious about a certain matter, stopped the prime minister, Hasan Muimandi, as he was leaving the royal presence.

'What did the sultan say?' they asked.

'Surely you know all about it?'

'The sultan tells you what he wouldn't reveal to the likes of us.'

'Precisely. And he does so because he knows that I will not reveal it. I don't know why you bother asking. Do you think I want to lose my job – and my head?'

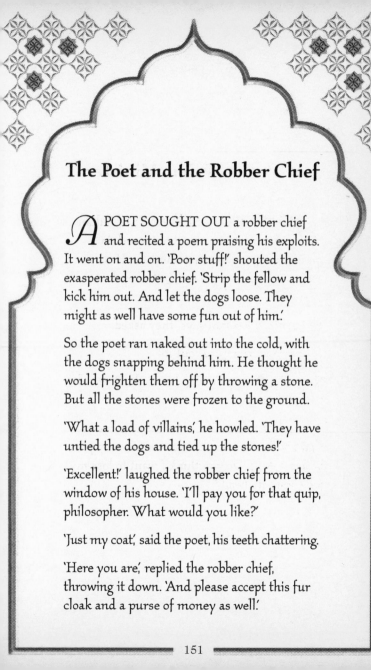

The Poet and the Robber Chief

A POET SOUGHT OUT a robber chief and recited a poem praising his exploits. It went on and on. 'Poor stuff!' shouted the exasperated robber chief. 'Strip the fellow and kick him out. And let the dogs loose. They might as well have some fun out of him.'

So the poet ran naked out into the cold, with the dogs snapping behind him. He thought he would frighten them off by throwing a stone. But all the stones were frozen to the ground.

'What a load of villains,' he howled. 'They have untied the dogs and tied up the stones!'

'Excellent!' laughed the robber chief from the window of his house. 'I'll pay you for that quip, philosopher. What would you like?'

'Just my coat,' said the poet, his teeth chattering.

'Here you are,' replied the robber chief, throwing it down. 'And please accept this fur cloak and a purse of money as well.'

It's Not What You Read . . .

A man with an unattractive rasping voice was loudly reciting the Koran when a wise man happened to pass by. He interrupted:

'How much are you being paid for this?'

'Nothing.'

'Then why are you doing it?'

'For the sake of God.'

'Then, for God's sake, I beg you to stop.'

The Final Lesson

... and other tales about pupils and masters, children and parents

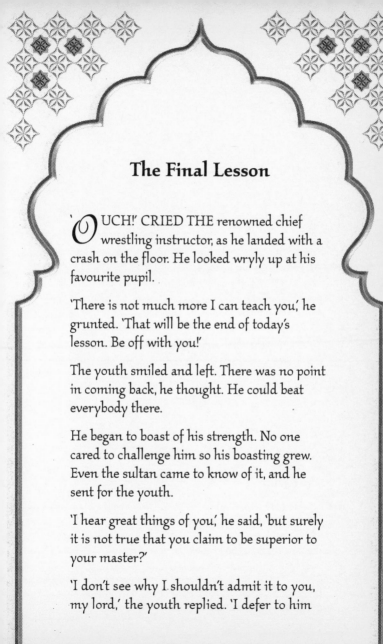

The Final Lesson

'*O*UCH!' CRIED THE renowned chief wrestling instructor, as he landed with a crash on the floor. He looked wryly up at his favourite pupil.

'There is not much more I can teach you,' he grunted. 'That will be the end of today's lesson. Be off with you!'

The youth smiled and left. There was no point in coming back, he thought. He could beat everybody there.

He began to boast of his strength. No one cared to challenge him so his boasting grew. Even the sultan came to know of it, and he sent for the youth.

'I hear great things of you,' he said, 'but surely it is not true that you claim to be superior to your master?'

'I don't see why I shouldn't admit it to you, my lord,' the youth replied. 'I defer to him

155

THE
DISCONTENTED DERVISHES

because of his age, of course. And I suppose I must be grateful for what skills he has taught. But I know now that I'm more than his equal.'

The sultan thought that this was disrespectful.

'We'll have a public contest, then,' he said, 'you versus your master.'

There was so much interest in the event that it had to be held in the largest arena. On the selected day the sultan and the whole of his court, and the people who had come from miles around, packed it to capacity.

The chief wrestling instructor stood in the middle of the arena, but all eyes fastened on the youth. He made a spectacular entrance and charged at once like a mad elephant – everyone could see that the impact would shift a mountain made of iron.

But the instructor stood calmly. Only at the very last moment did he quickly catch hold of the youth in a way that no one could clearly see. But everyone saw the result.

With a howl of pain the youth flew up in the air and was thrown down with an agonising thump that was felt all over the arena.

A roar of applause and delight went up. The sultan embraced the instructor, placed the robe of honour upon him, and gave him many presents.

'So,' he said to the still groaning youth, 'this is what comes of presuming to tackle your master!'

'It was a trick!' the youth protested, 'and one that he never taught me. That's how he did it, not by strength.'

The instructor said to the sultan: 'I am thankful that I was able to heed the saying: Even your best friend may one day be an enemy.'

To his pupil he said: 'I am master of three hundred and sixty tricks and because of the love I bore you I taught you three hundred and fifty nine of them. One only I kept for myself, for an occasion such as this.'

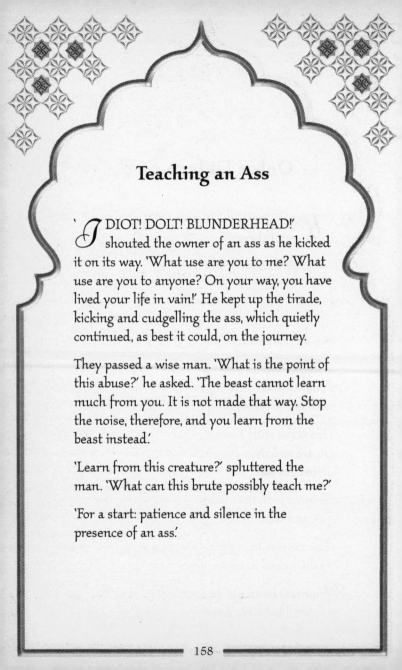

Teaching an Ass

'IDIOT! DOLT! BLUNDERHEAD!' shouted the owner of an ass as he kicked it on its way. 'What use are you to me? What use are you to anyone? On your way, you have lived your life in vain!' He kept up the tirade, kicking and cudgelling the ass, which quietly continued, as best it could, on the journey.

They passed a wise man. 'What is the point of this abuse?' he asked. 'The beast cannot learn much from you. It is not made that way. Stop the noise, therefore, and you learn from the beast instead.'

'Learn from this creature?' spluttered the man. 'What can this brute possibly teach me?'

'For a start: patience and silence in the presence of an ass.'

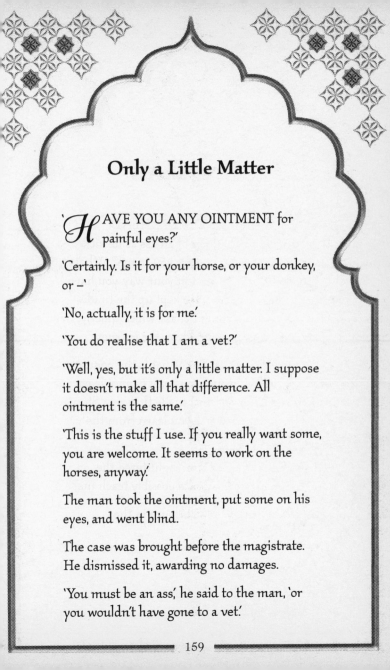

Only a Little Matter

'*H*AVE YOU ANY OINTMENT for painful eyes?'

'Certainly. Is it for your horse, or your donkey, or –'

'No, actually, it is for me.'

'You do realise that I am a vet?'

'Well, yes, but it's only a little matter. I suppose it doesn't make all that difference. All ointment is the same.'

'This is the stuff I use. If you really want some, you are welcome. It seems to work on the horses, anyway.'

The man took the ointment, put some on his eyes, and went blind.

The case was brought before the magistrate. He dismissed it, awarding no damages.

'You must be an ass,' he said to the man, 'or you wouldn't have gone to a vet.'

The Scorpion

THEY ASKED A SCORPION: 'Why don't you come out in the winter?'

'You must be joking!' it replied. 'I have just spent all summer hiding from your sticks, evading your traps, shrinking from your stamping feet, scurrying even from your dogs. Do you really expect me to come out in the winter as well?'

Educating the Prince

A KING SOUGHT OUT the tutor with the best reputation in his kingdom, and said:

'I propose to entrust my son to you.'

The tutor bowed. 'I am honoured,' he said. 'I have sons of his age. Would it be acceptable to you, my lord, if I put the prince among them, and educated him as if he were my own son?'

'An excellent arrangement,' the king replied.

After several years, the prince was returned. He did not appear to have learned anything, while the tutor's sons were renowned throughout the land for the excellence of their scholastic achievement.

In anger, the king sent for the tutor.

'What is the meaning of this?' he asked. 'You have not done as we agreed.'

The tutor replied: 'My lord, all the boys under my care got exactly the same education. It was their capacities that differed.'

The Good Schoolmaster

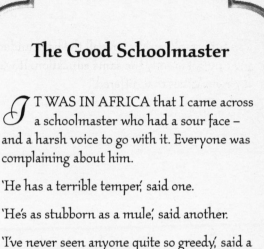

I T WAS IN AFRICA that I came across a schoolmaster who had a sour face – and a harsh voice to go with it. Everyone was complaining about him.

'He has a terrible temper,' said one.

'He's as stubborn as a mule,' said another.

'I've never seen anyone quite so greedy,' said a third.

'I can't bear the sight of him, he's so untidy,' said a fourth. A fifth added:

'Do you want to be depressed? Go and hear him reading the Koran!'

And these were the adults! What about the children?

It was pitiful to see innocent girls and boys under the daily tyranny of this monster. All laughter and merriment, all childhood chatter, died when he was about. He regularly boxed

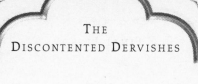

their ears. It was common to see boys under-
going the agony of the stocks. What misery
they suffered.

At last the people decided they could put up
with it no longer. They got some definite
evidence of bad behaviour and had him taken
to court. He was convicted, ordered to be
beaten, and of course he lost his job.

'That's a relief!' everyone said.

'Now, we must appoint another schoolmaster.
I know just the man . . .'

What a contrast the new schoolmaster was.

'Such a gentle person.'

'Goodness itself.'

'Have you noticed – he never says an
unnecessary word?'

'He's religious . . . makes all the difference.'

And the children liked him. He was never
harsh with them. He was always kind. With
this angel in front of them they quickly forgot

the terrors of the demon they had had before.

However, the odd thing was that the children themselves began to change. They neglected their studies, but this didn't matter because the schoolmaster was just as kind and gentle as before, and never told them off. And then, when they began to play about in class, he just carried on, quietly speaking and smiling.

Things went from bad to worse. Soon the place was in an uproar and the children were like demons. Yes, they used their wooden copying boards – to break upon each other's heads!

It was plain that things could not go on like this. Within a fortnight, calm was restored, and peace returned. How was it done? They got the old schoolmaster back. They placated him somehow (at considerable expense, I would think) and begged him to return.

I passed the schoolroom and saw him once more in control.

'That demon's back in charge of the angels again.' I said.

An old man of wide experience, sitting in peace at the door, smiled and said:

'Have you heard about the king who, on the first day his son went to school, gave him a silver medallion to wear? On it, in golden letters, was written: A fond father is more harmful than a severe teacher.'

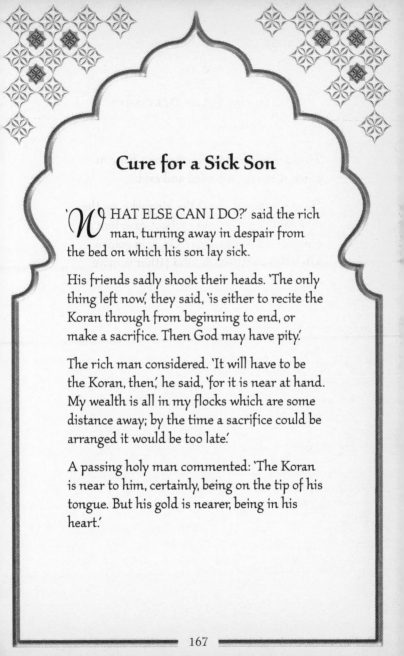

Cure for a Sick Son

'WHAT ELSE CAN I DO?' said the rich man, turning away in despair from the bed on which his son lay sick.

His friends sadly shook their heads. 'The only thing left now,' they said, 'is either to recite the Koran through from beginning to end, or make a sacrifice. Then God may have pity.'

The rich man considered. 'It will have to be the Koran, then,' he said, 'for it is near at hand. My wealth is all in my flocks which are some distance away; by the time a sacrifice could be arranged it would be too late.'

A passing holy man commented: 'The Koran is near to him, certainly, being on the tip of his tongue. But his gold is nearer, being in his heart.'

The Wishing Tree

I WAS ONCE THE GUEST of a rich old man who had a handsome son.

'He is the only son I ever had,' he told me. He went on to relate that there was a tree in a certain valley to which pilgrims went to make petitions and pray for what they wanted.

'I made my pilgrimage,' he said, and spent night after night at the foot of that tree, weeping and beseeching the Almighty to give me a son. And, see, He heard me in the end, and granted my desire!'

I overheard the boy whisper to his companion: 'O, if I knew where that tree was! I would pray there for the old fool's death.'

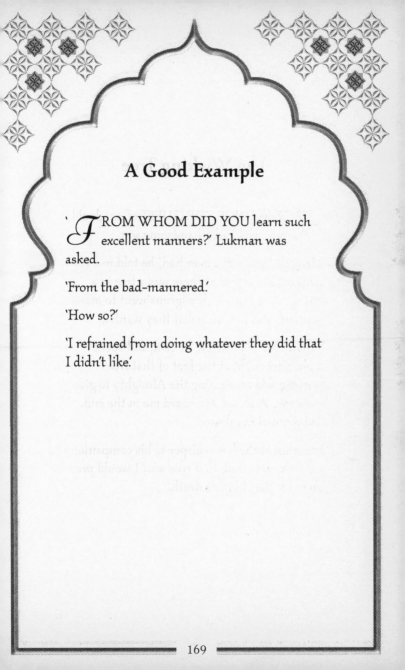

A Good Example

'*F*ROM WHOM DID YOU learn such excellent manners?' Lukman was asked.

'From the bad-mannered.'

'How so?'

'I refrained from doing whatever they did that I didn't like.'

Better to Sleep

I REMEMBER THAT ONCE, when a child, I went through a holy phase. I fasted, and I used to get up in the night to pray. Once, I sat up all night with my father. I held the sacred Koran in my lap and never once closed my eyes.

All around us the rest of the household snored in sleep.

'Just listen to them,' I remarked to my father, 'Not one of them thinks of saying a prayer. They are sleeping like the dead.'

'My beloved son,' he replied, 'you would be much better asleep yourself if all you can do in your wakefulness is disparage others.'

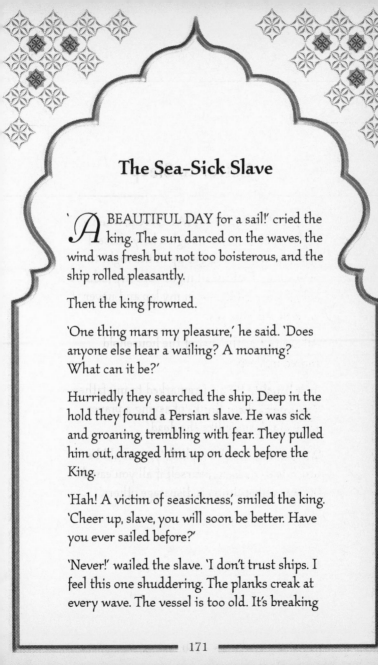

The Sea-Sick Slave

'*A* BEAUTIFUL DAY for a sail!' cried the king. The sun danced on the waves, the wind was fresh but not too boisterous, and the ship rolled pleasantly.

Then the king frowned.

'One thing mars my pleasure,' he said. 'Does anyone else hear a wailing? A moaning? What can it be?'

Hurriedly they searched the ship. Deep in the hold they found a Persian slave. He was sick and groaning, trembling with fear. They pulled him out, dragged him up on deck before the King.

'Hah! A victim of seasickness,' smiled the king. 'Cheer up, slave, you will soon be better. Have you ever sailed before?'

'Never!' wailed the slave. 'I don't trust ships. I feel this one shuddering. The planks creak at every wave. The vessel is too old. It's breaking

up!' He sank to the deck, gibbering with terror.

'Nonsense!' laughed the king. 'This is a new ship. Don't worry, you will soon recover and then you will enjoy the voyage, like me.'

The slave went on wailing.

'Oh, take him below again', said the king. 'See what you can do for him. But do keep him quiet. I want to enjoy the trip, if he doesn't!'

All night the slave howled. Next morning he could still be heard all over the ship.

After a sleepless night the king had lost all his patience.

'Tell him I shall have him whipped!' he shouted.

The wails became louder.

'Threaten him with red hot irons!'

It made no difference. The king was thoroughly exasperated.

Eventually another passenger, a philosopher, bowed before the king.

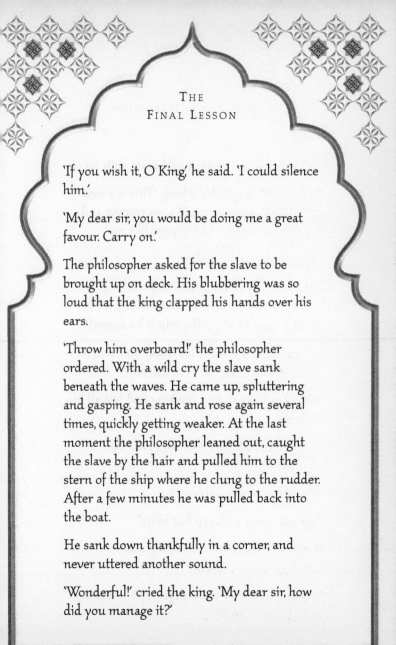

'If you wish it, O King,' he said. 'I could silence him.'

'My dear sir, you would be doing me a great favour. Carry on.'

The philosopher asked for the slave to be brought up on deck. His blubbering was so loud that the king clapped his hands over his ears.

'Throw him overboard!' the philosopher ordered. With a wild cry the slave sank beneath the waves. He came up, spluttering and gasping. He sank and rose again several times, quickly getting weaker. At the last moment the philosopher leaned out, caught the slave by the hair and pulled him to the stern of the ship where he clung to the rudder. After a few minutes he was pulled back into the boat.

He sank down thankfully in a corner, and never uttered another sound.

'Wonderful!' cried the king. 'My dear sir, how did you manage it?'

'There is nothing like a calamity to help us appreciate good times,' the philosopher replied. 'I knew he had only to taste the agony of drowning and he would appreciate the ship as he had never done before!'

A Dirty Mouth

WHEN I WAS YOUNG I once wanted to fast for the sake of my religious beliefs. I knew that I had to go through some sort of ritual cleansing beforehand and, as I didn't know how to do this, I called on a holy man who lived in the village.

'My boy,' he said, 'you couldn't have come to a better person. I know all there is to know about this sort of thing. Sit down, and I'll soon have you on the right path.

'First then – and all this is according to the Law of the Prophet, you know – you begin by repeating: "In the Name of God." Have you got that?

'Having done this you can go on to the washing of the mouth and the nose, using your little finger like this to ensure that your nostrils are clean.

'Then you rub your front teeth with your forefinger, so, for after sunset the rules are so

strict that it is forbidden to touch your lips
even with a toothbrush.

'Next you splash your face three times with a
handful of water, making sure that the water
covers from the top of your forehead, here
where the hair begins, down to your chin.

'Now, again you wash your hands, and your
arms up to the elbow, at the same time
reciting all you know in praise of the Name of
God.

'Following this you must again wipe your
head, finally washing your feet.

'Then conclude, as you began, with another
"In the Name of God".

'And that's it. As I said, if ever you are in
doubt, come to me. I'm an expert in such
things.'

It was at this point, I recall, that the head man
of the village slowly walked past the door.

'Decrepit old fool', muttered the holy man.

The head man stopped and turned.

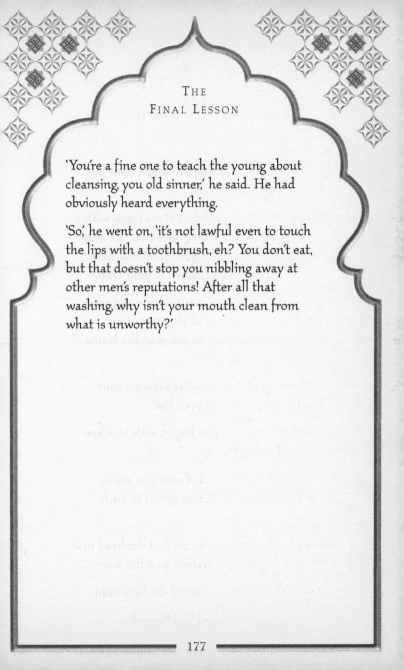

THE
FINAL LESSON

'You're a fine one to teach the young about cleansing, you old sinner,' he said. He had obviously heard everything.

'So,' he went on, 'it's not lawful even to touch the lips with a toothbrush, eh? You don't eat, but that doesn't stop you nibbling away at other men's reputations! After all that washing, why isn't your mouth clean from what is unworthy?'

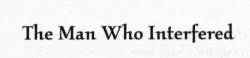

The Man Who Interfered

$\mathcal{J}$T WAS IN INDIA, said a wise old man, that I suddenly turned a corner to see a white girl being embraced by a black man. He was on top of her and clasping her so tightly that I could see that she was almost smothered. It was as if night were covering day.

Well, I thought, I'd better try and do something to help the girl if I can. I hunted round, found a stick and belaboured the man with it, shouting:

'Godless one! Nameless! Shameless!'

I kept up the shouting and the beating until suddenly he ran off across the garden. It was as if night had fled before the dawn. The girl lay there like an egg, discovered after the crow had flown.

And now, I thought, she will show me some sign of gratitude.

Not a bit of it! Up she jumped and grabbed my robe.

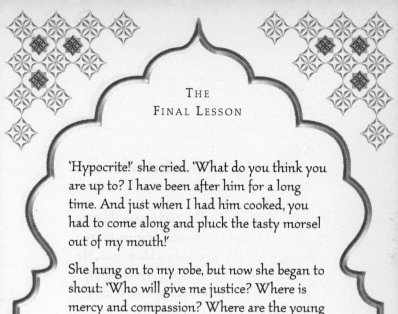

'Hypocrite!' she cried. 'What do you think you are up to? I have been after him for a long time. And just when I had him cooked, you had to come along and pluck the tasty morsel out of my mouth!'

She hung on to my robe, but now she began to shout: 'Who will give me justice? Where is mercy and compassion? Where are the young men to rescue such as me from tyrants like this?'

I did not know what to do. I hid my face for shame in my robe. A crowd began to gather. There was nothing for it but to slip out of my robe and run off naked.

I lost the robe but it was worth it.

Sometime later I opened by door and there stood the girl!

'Do you know me?' she demanded.

'I've repented!' I cried. 'You've taught me a lesson. Believe me, I won't interfere again!'

The Prisoner

KING AZUD'S SON had been ill for some time, and the king was losing his patience.

'Try setting free all the caged birds,' someone advised.

The king went into the garden, and threw all the cages open. With a flurry of wings the birds were gone. Only one bird did the king keep. This was his famous sweet-singing nightingale, in a special cage which hung from the arch of the summerhouse.

Next morning the prince rushed into the garden to find the birds gone. But when he saw the nightingale, he smiled sadly.

'You, too, would have been free,' he said, 'if you did not have such a beautiful voice.'

A Heavy Tomb

J ONCE SAW THE SON of a rich man,
sitting on the magnificent tomb of his
father. He was quarrelling with another boy,
the son of a dervish, and saying:

'Look at the splendour of my father's tomb.
See the marble pavements, the turquoise
bricks! And inside, the stone coffin is covered
with an elegant epitaph. Compare all this to
your father's grave – a couple of bricks
sprinkled with dust!'

The dervish boy listened and said:

'By the time your father has been able to get
out from under there, mine will long have
been in Paradise.'

The Secret of Knowledge

*T*HE WELL-KNOWN AUTHOR and spiritual guide, the Imam Murshid Muhammed Ghazali, was asked how he had been able to become so knowledgeable.

He replied:

'I was never ashamed to ask whatever I did not know.'

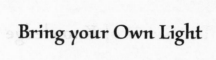

Bring your Own Light

MY YOUNG SON DIED in Sina.

What can I tell you of my sorrow? The boy was like a young cypress, his roots plucked up by the wind of death. All I could say in my heart was: He has gone pure to God, whereas I, an old man, go stained.

Mad with distress one day, I went to his tomb and pulled up a stone. Inside, all was narrow, oppressive and dark. I shrank back in fear and confusion.

In that sad state I seemed to hear the voice of my beloved son:

'Father, are you afraid of this dark place? Be wise then and bring your own light in with you. Do you wish the night of the grave to be as day? Out there in the world, then, kindle a lamp of good deeds.'